DPMax

A Tool for Textual and Graphical Analyses of Common Dynamic Programming Algorithms.

CHRISTIAN COLOSSUS

GRADUATE DIPLOMA THESIS
BIOINFORMATICS FOR SOFTWARE PROFESSIONALS PROGRAM
CENTENNIAL COLLEGE, TORONTO

SECOND EDITION

ISBN: 9781794761100

Copyright (c) 2019 All Rights Reserved

First Edition Spring 2009

Part 1

The Longest Common Subsequence

ABSTRACT

DPMax (*Dynamic Programming to the Max*) is a software tool based on the dynamic programming (DP) algorithmic technique, which is a technique employed for solving certain kinds of computational problems. DPMax is a software program comprising various modules of algorithms that employ dynamic programming to solve their particular problems. The primary focus of the original version of DPMax (DPMax version 1.0) is on the techniques of *Longest Common Subsequence* (LCS) and *Longest/Shortest Paths Problem Using Graph Weights*. Of these two, the focus of this paper is the LCS module, which comprises the Input, Output and Graphics tabs. The Weights module is detailed in the second part of this paper. The current version of the DPMax software, version 1.0.1, makes no changes to the functionality of the modules. It only makes slight changes to the graphical user interface.

DPMax for LCS (*Longest Common Subsequence for Dynamic Programming*) simplifies the LCS process by providing both textual and graphical presentations of the solution of the problem being solved by the algorithm. Its textual output presents the solution to the LCS in a textual format. After solving the problem, the program also provides a graphical presentation of the solution of the LCS. The graphical output tab provides a visual display of the LCS solution.

DPMax for Weights also makes the function of achieving the longest and shortest paths easy to comprehend with its text and graphic outputs. The text output with weights displays the pairs of rows-columns which represent the vertices of the graph used to display the graphical solution.

DPMax provides a deeper understanding of both the Weights and LCS techniques. The combination of the text and graphical presentations of the solution make it easier to see and appreciate what problem has been solved and how that solution was achieved.

However, the original intention of DPMax 1.0 was not only to present the two types of DP techniques already mentioned. Version 1.0 was written to be a combination of various classic algorithmic techniques that apply DP in finding the solutions to the problems they solve. Since the program lists the modules originally intended for the full program, I will mention each one briefly.

Weights: This is the DP technique that solves the problem of finding the shortest/longest distances between 2 points using the weights of the edges of the graphs of the distances between the 2 points as explained in the *Manhattan Tourist Problem* (Dasgupta, et. al., Reingold et. al.).

LCS: This is the DP technique that solves the problem of the *Longest Common Subsequence* between 2 given nucleotide sequences. It is one of a list of common string algorithms that apply dynamic programming (Cormen et. al., Chapter 15, Chong et. al., Dasgupta, et. al., Chapter 6).

Rocks: This is the DP algorithm that solves the *Rocks* games (Dasgupta et. al.).

Global Sequence Alignment: This is the DP technique applied to find the alignment between the entireties of two sequences using a particular scoring matrix. It is also known as *Needleman-Wunsch* alignment after the two scientists, Needleman and Wunsch, who formulated it. The algorithm was developed by Saul Needleman and Christian Wunsch and published in 1970. (Needleman and Wunsch, 1970)

Local Sequence Alignment: This is the DP algorithm that solves alignment of local areas within 2 sequences that may have similarities. It finds the local alignments of sequences and is a modification of the Needleman-Wunsch global alignment algorithm. It was proposed by Temple Smith and Michael Waterman in 1981, and is known as the *Smith-Waterman* algorithm (Smith and Waterman)

Sequence Alignment with Gaps: This is the alignment of sequences using algorithms that employ gaps (Mount).

Multiple Sequence Alignment: This is the DP algorithm that solves the alignments of 2 or more sequences with the same lengths. The worst-case runtime here is N^m where N is the number of sequences and m is the common length of all N sequences (Mount, Dasgupta, et. al.).

Multi-Dimensional: This is the DP algorithm that solves problems using the alignment of multiple sequences with different lengths. The typical worst-case runtime here is simply the product of the lengths of the various sequences (Mount).

After its creation, DPMax for LCS was used to determine the LCS between pairs of nucleotide and peptide sequences. The result for one pair of peptides is presented here. The software was also used for the determination of the longest paths between points input by a user using the Weights algorithm. Those results are presented in the paper on the Weights algorithm.

INTRODUCTION

What is Dynamic Programming

Dynamic programming (DP) is a technique for the design of algorithms that enables computational problems to be solved in polynomial time. It is a proven technique for solving problems whose solutions require optimization. Optimization is any process that produces the end-result of the maximum or minimum value for any given problem. Anytime the maximum or minimum value is required as the solution for any given problem, then that problem is an optimization problem. Optimization problems are those which generally follow the principle of optimality as proposed by the inventor of dynamic programming, Richard Bellman (Bellman, p. 83). This principle states that:

An optimal policy has the property that whatever the initial states and initial decisions are, the remaining decisions must constitute an optimal policy with regard to the state resulting from the first decision.

In other words, *Every optimal policy must comprise only optimal subpolicies* (Cooper and Cooper). Many DP solutions run in polynomial times of $O(N^2)$ or $O(N^3)$ rather than the exponential (2^N) or other non-polynomial (NP) times that would result otherwise using brute force or other naïve approaches. DP simplifies computationally intensive tasks using its unique design techniques that avoid redundancies in producing a solution. It achieves this by breaking a problem into a series of smaller problems, with each problem having similar variables, or input parameters, that must be solved in order to move on to the next problem in the series and solve that one. Each problem in the series can be solved using the same function, and hence the multi-stage solution is referred to as a *recurrence*. By the time the last element in the multi-stage series is solved, the solution to the main problem would have already been achieved. Although it is not the only approach to optimization problems, it is an immensely popular technique in the fields of Mathematics, Bioinformatics and Computer Science.

There are two characteristic features of problems that may indicate they can be solved by DP:

1. Overlapping sub-problems: Many optimization problems can be decomposed into smaller problems – sub-problems – each of which can be solved by the same recursive algorithm. The combined solution of all those sub-problems becomes the solution of the main problem. These subproblems can be seen to be interrelated, with each one connected to every other one through its closest relatives. These 'overlapping,' or 'interrelated' sub-problems can be solved one after the other until all have been solved and a final solution to the main problem is found. DP is a way to solve the main problem by solving each of its smaller, overlapping sub-problems. In the absence of the overlapping property, a non-DP routine such as divide-and-conquer would suffice to solve the sub-problems.

2. Optimal substructure: If the optimal solution to the main problem can be found from optimal solutions to its sub-problems, then that decomposed structure of the main problem, as expressed by its sub-problems, can be described as an optimal substructure. Optimization techniques can be applied to solve the smaller problems and produce global or local optima, that is, local or global minimum or maximum values. DP uses techniques that eliminate all redundancies in solving this unique substructure, and thereby reduces the computation time from exponential to polynomial.

The 2 properties above are the classic properties of DP solvability or applicability. But I shall now introduce a 3rd one, something I call the *DP Matrix Test*. This property is presented graphically in Figure 1 as a decision tree. Try and visualize the problem in your mind or diagrammatically on paper. If you can see the problem as a matrix of smaller problems which can all be solved in the same way regardless of the variables that need to be computed to achieve each solution, then you probably have a good DP candidate. If both of the criteria above have been met and the solution to the problem would result in a maximum or minimum value or score, then it is a confirmation that the problem can most probably be solved by DP. For instance, applications to find the shortest path between two points in a city, or the longest common subsequence between 2 strings or sequences, are good prospective applications of DP. Another one is the minimization of transaction costs in a business venture.

Before I proceed in this discussion, I must present my definition of a DP Matrix. A DP Matrix is an array of arrays of objects – in this case subproblems of a larger problem – which can be arranged in series, or sequentially, with each one having the same or very similar properties like inputs needed to produce a solution, and outputs after the solution has been produced. Each object in the matrix must therefore be connected to the one in front of it by the same or an increasing factor and also to the one behind it by the same or a decreasing factor in the progression towards the array. If the smaller pieces of the puzzle, that is, the main problem, can be broken down as in the case of the Fibonacci series, then they should be visualized in a matrix, just like pieces of a puzzle.

These 3 properties above take a good amount of practice and experience to master, but with time good DP skills can certainly be achieved. It should be noted that in the field of Bioinformatics, many DP algorithms produce the maximization, or minimization, of some value such as a score or a cost.

Dynamic Programming algorithms are built using one of 2 different methods:

    1. Top-Down Method: This starts from the main problem and divides it into smaller sub-problems using recursion.

It then recurses through the smaller problems while solving each one of them until it gets to, and solves, the smallest sub-problem, and then it stops. By this time, it has found the optimal solution of the main problem. It starts from the top, i.e. the main problem, and works its way to the bottom. It employs a technique called *memoization* to remember its optimal solutions due to the inefficiency of its recursion. For instance, to solve the 7th number in the Fibonacci series, this method would start with the 7th number and proceed downwards the smaller numbers until it gets to 0. That is, it would solve Fib(7), then Fib(6) then Fib(5) until it gets to the base cases of F(1) and F(0).

2. Bottom-Up Method: This method moves in the opposite direction of the top-down method. In contrast to the top-down method, it starts with the smallest sub-problem. It then solves the smaller sub-problems while using their solutions to solve the bigger sub-problems. It keeps on doing this until it reaches and solves the largest of the sub-problems and at that point it would have found the optimal solution to the main problem. Like the top-down method, there is also a need to store its own solutions. But, a table-like data structure is often employed here and hence this method is sometimes called the *Tabulation* method (GeeksforGeeks, Cormen et. al.). It typically leads to the creation of multi-dimensional array matrixes in its quest for a solution. It starts from the bottom and works its way gradually to the top. The bottom-up method is the method used throughout this project and is my preferred DP method. For instance, to solve the 7th number in the Fibonacci series, this method would start with the smallest, the 0th number and proceed upwards through the larger numbers until it gets to 7. That is, it would solve Fib(0), then Fib(1) then Fib(2) until it gets to F(7).

Let's assume we are to find the solution of the 9th number in the Fibonacci series. In the Fibonacci series, Fib(0) to Fib(9) can be arranged in a 3-by-3 matrix grid and then a recurrence to solve each one can be tested through each one to see if they can be solved by that recurrent function. Once all the small pieces can be resolved as interrelated via common properties, then there is overlap between them. If the same optimization function can be applied to each one to solve them, then surely DP can be employed as a technique to solve the main problem at hand and even larger instances of the problem.

Figure 1: The choice of Dynamic Programming represented as a decision tree.

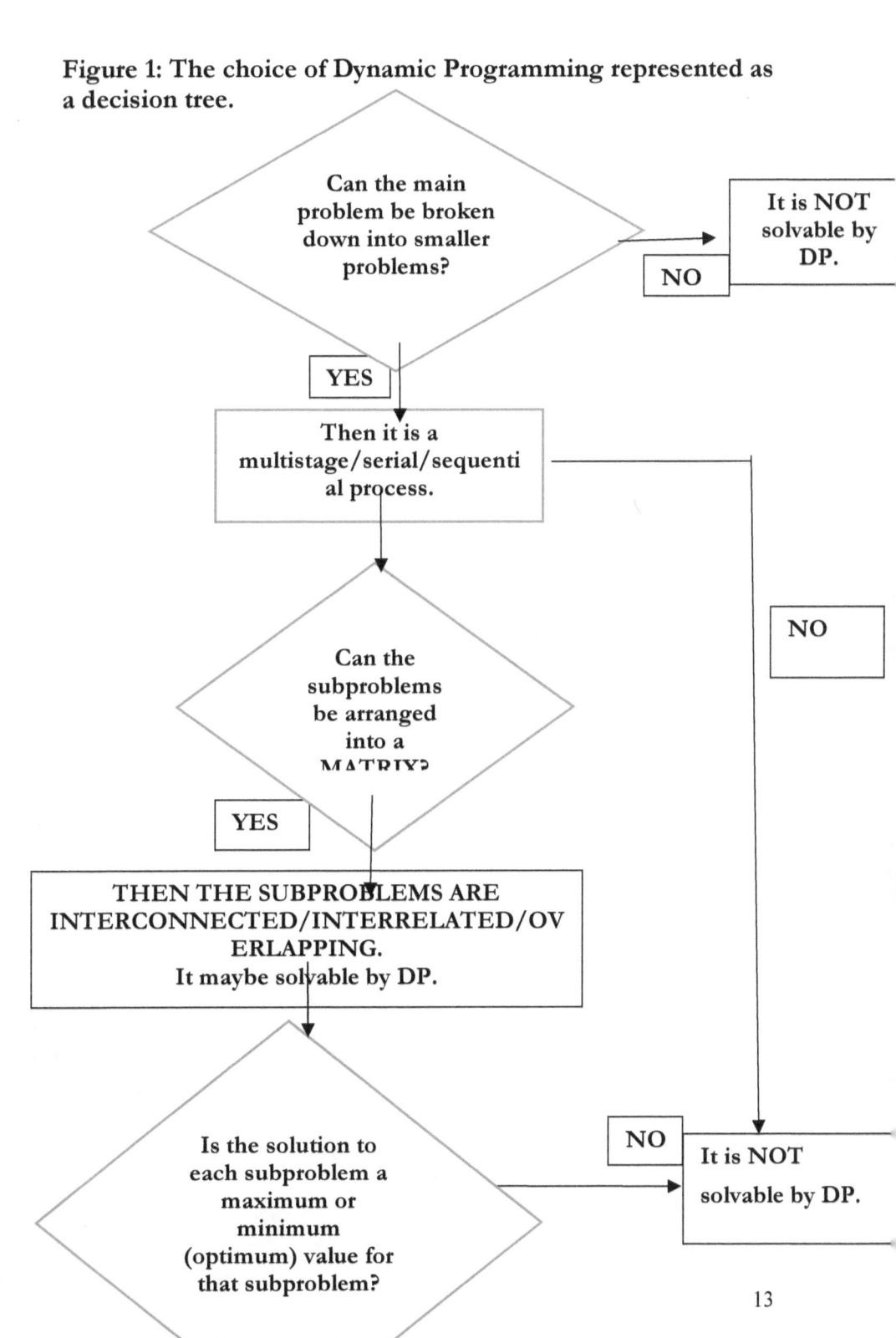

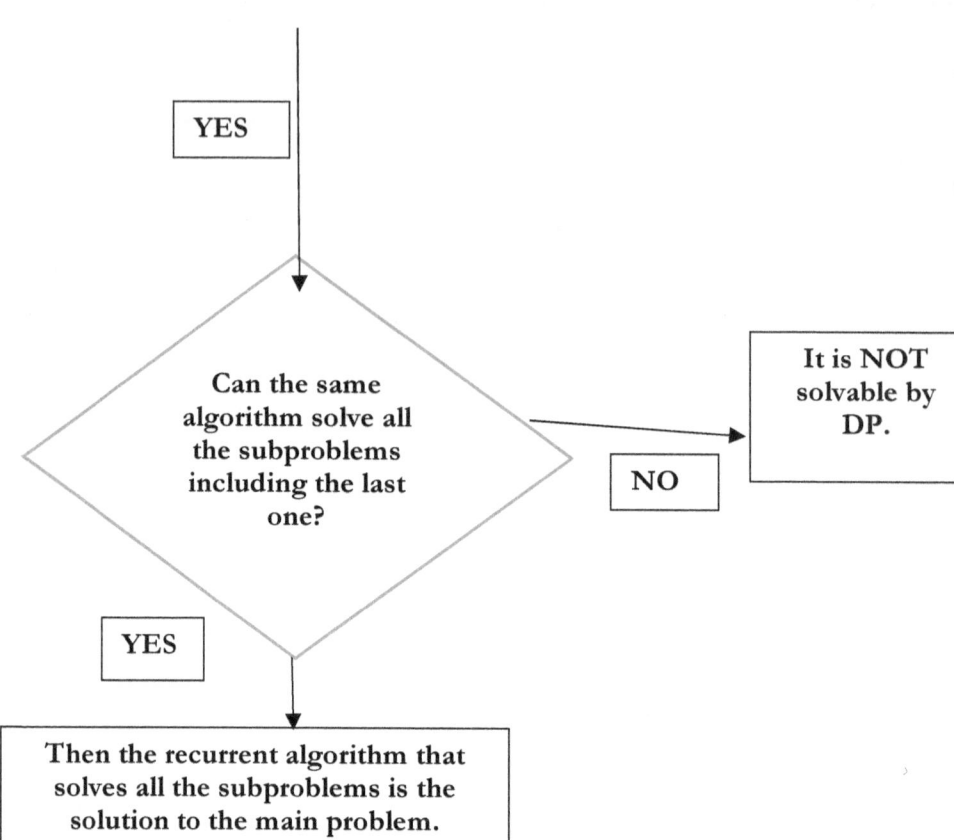

How to Find the Solutions to A Problem Using Dynamic Programming

There are usually 4 main considerations to finding a solution to a problem using Dynamic Programming.

1. Identification of an Optimal Problem Solvable by DP:

The first step to solving any problem is to apply the 3 steps listed above that identify problems that can be solved using the technique of DP. There should be a clear indication of the Bellman's principle of optimality. Furthermore, the main problem which may not contain a large number of related variables should be seen as one problem which is made up of smaller problems, and these subproblems should be solvable by solving for one or a few variables. (Cooper and Cooper, p. 9). In other words, the main problem must consist only of optimal subproblems. Once DP has been chosen as the technique to be applied to obtain the solution, the next step must be taken to formulate an actual solution.

2. Analysis and Design of a Suitable DP Algorithm

The second step is to find the perfect algorithm that can solve each subproblem. This algorithm is commonly a recursive algorithm (a recurrence) that will be applied to all smaller problems to attain the optimal solution of the main problem. The recurrence can be applied using one of the 2 methods – top-down or bottom-up. This recurrent algorithm is often built using the classic top-down approach as can be observed in most DP implementations. But to avoid the recursion in its implementation, it may be useful to create a bottom-up expression of the top-down algorithm. Then the code can be implemented using that bottom-up approach.

3. Storage of The Solution to Subproblems.

A lot of the successes of DP techniques lie in the choice of storing the solution to each subproblem as each one of them is being solved. It is from this store that the solutions to the next subproblems in the series can be computed. It is also due to this store that there are no redundancies that can lead to exponential run-times. This store can be a class member variable, a simple array, a map or some other data structure that can be stored in program memory. In this LCS bottom-up implementation, every cell in the 2-Dimensional array matrix has its own Map object which not only stores its solution but also how that solution was achieved, the cell/s which produced that solution, and a list of all its surrounding cells. No successful DP algorithm can do without storing its solutions during iteration. A well-designed algorithm is incomplete without this memory store (Baase and van Gelder).

4. Backtracking

Once the optimal solution has been found by solving through the optimal substructure, then the actual solution, which is the path to that optimal solution, must be obtained by walking backwards through the matrix structure. The backtracking from the top through to the bottom, or beginning to the end of the matrix.

As soon as the backtracking is complete, then the solution of the problem by the DP technique would practically have been achieved.

5. Test the Recursive and Backtracking Functions for an Acceptable Time Complexity

As soon as the backtracking has been achieved, the whole system with all its functions should be tested to ascertain the overall time complexity. If the runtime of the solution is not acceptable, then another recursive or backtracking functions should be found. Techniques such as parallelization should be implemented to obtain a more suitable runtime (Chong et. al.). Once there is a satisfactory runtime, then a true solution has been found.

Though dynamic programming has its great benefits, it also has its drawbacks. Its main drawback results from one of its strengths. Due to the need to store its solutions in memory using either approach, it uses a large amount of space. Giving a large amount of input, this can easily become one of the constraints of the program (Skiena).

What is the Longest Common Subsequence?

The Longest Common Subsequence (LCS) between two given sequences, A and B, is the longest common subsequence formed by the characters common to both sequences in the set of sequences.

Let us start by defining the algorithm for the LCS function between A and B, LCS(A, B).

$A = (A_1, A_2, A_3, \ldots, A_N)$,

$B = (B_1, B_2, B_3, \ldots, B_M)$,

Where,

N is the number of rows, and

M is the number of columns

We may define the recursive relation as:

If (i = 0 or j = 0)

$\quad$ LCS $(A_i, B_j) = 0$ $\qquad$ (the initialization in the relation)

$\qquad\qquad\qquad\qquad\qquad$ (1)

If $(A_i = B_j)$

$\quad$ LCS $(A_i, B_j) = 1 +$ LCS (A_{i-1}, B_{j-1})

$\qquad\qquad\qquad\qquad$ (2)

$\quad$ //Add 1 to the score of the upper-left diagonal to give you

$\quad$ //the score of the current cell

Else

$\quad$ LCS $(A_i, B_j) =$ Max (LCS(A_{i-1}, B_j), LCS(A_i, B_{j-1}))

$\qquad\qquad\qquad\qquad$ (3)

$\quad$ //the score of the current cell is the greater of the scores in the

$\quad$ //left and upper cells

Below is the Bottom-Up expression of the LCS algorithm (Cormen et. al., Chong *et. al.*)

```
function doLCS(S1, S2)  begin
   int n = length of first sequence, S1
   int m = length of second sequence, S2
   Array lcsArr = 2-Dimensional array of [n, m]
   //Initialize lcsArr elements to 0
   for i = 0 to n
      lcsArr[i, 0] = 0
   for j = 0 to m
      lcsArr[0, j] = 0

   for i = 1 to n        begin                                    (4)
      for j = 1 to m begin                                         (5)
         if a[i] = b[j] then
            lcsArr[i, j] = 1 + lcsArr[i-1, j-1]                    (6)
         else
            lcsArr[i, j] = max(lcsArr[i-1, j], lcsArr[i, j-1])     (7)
         endif
      end
   end
   return lcsArr[n, m]
end doLCS
```

Computational Complexity

The first algorithm is the general recursive relation of the LCS algorithm. From the algorithm above, the calls to LCS represent the 2-Dimensional array matrix since this is an implementation of the bottom-up DP method. As it has been previously noted, my preferred method is the bottom-up method. The initialization step sets the values in the matrix to 0 in the first row and first column. The total number of calls made through S1 is $O(n)$ which is the length of the first sequence. The same applies to the second sequence S2. For each loop through the characters of S1, there is a comparison to each character in S2, producing a runtime of $O(m)$ for the total calls made through S2. This means that we loop through our total number of subproblems of $O(n)$ by $O(m)$ equaling $O(nm)$.

It should be noted that all the 3 lines in the LCS algorithm and 4 lines in the bottom-up expression above are occurring through the array as each subproblem is being solved. Lines (4) and (5) have the 2 loops where the $O(mn)$ cost is being produced. Lines (2) and (6) are where we have a match and lines (3) and (7) occur when there is a mismatch between the characters of both sequences. If there is a match, we simply take the value in the upper left cell/subproblem and increment it by 1, a mere addition operation. Otherwise, if there is a mismatch, we take the maximum between the left and upper subproblems/cells and use that as the solution to the current subproblem. This too is a simple constant maximum-of-two operation. Whichever the case, both operations result in a basic operation through the matrix to solve each subproblem that costs a constant time of only $O(1)$.

Therefore, the total runtime through the matrix is the time it takes to go through the matrix of subproblems multiplied by the basic operation time. This come out to $O(nm)$ x $O(1)$ which is $O(nm)$. Due to the need to store all its solutions in a table, the space complexity is also $O(nm)$.

It should be noted here that a simple Min() or Max() function in both the Weights (comparing the left and upper vertices) and LCS (comparing the left and upper cells in a mismatch) algorithms would not be sufficient in producing the numerous path solutions that may exist in both matrixes. Such naïve implementations would certainly produce only one path to the optimal solution even if there exists more than one. Care must be taken to ensure that if there are equal values in the graph vertices or in the case of an LCS mismatch, they both should be indicated as producing the solution to the current vertex or cell.

METHODS AND EXPERIMENTS

The goal of the project required development of software that would solve common problems in the field of Bioinformatics (aka *Computational Molecular Biology*, aka *Computational Biology*) using dynamic programming. The method uses Java 5/Java 6 Graphics and Graphics2D APIs to build graphic displays of the DP matrix showing how the matrix was solved. This was done by showing graphically the matrix with each cell with the solution(s) of each cell and how that cell was solved. The cell solutions are displayed in 2 parts –

1. The number that was the solution for that cell, and,

2. Arrows showing which of the three possible methods that produced the current cell's solution –

a.) An arrow pointing to the cell above and towards the sequence on the horizontal (S2) indicating that it is where the solution of the current cell came from,

b.) An arrow pointing to the cell on the left of the current cell at the sequence on the vertical indicating the solution came from S1, and,

c.) An arrow pointing to the left upper diagonal indicating a match of the characters of both sequences.

It should be made very clear that the arrows are primarily backtracking pointers which should enable a successful traceback. The first two directions of arrows in (a) and (b) above both indicate a mismatch between the characters of the two sequences. The arrows point in the direction of the origin of the matrix, $Z[0, 0]$, and pointing away from the final cell in the position $Z[A_n, B_m]$, that is, $Z[nRows_{-1}, nCols_{-1}]$. Actually, the first characters begin in the first row and first column, and this is where the backtracking operation will end.

As such, there may be multiple arrows in any given cell signifying that the cell has more than one solution. In this way, a visual traceback can be performed by any user to obtain a solution from the optimal cell through the matrix to the origin cell at position $Z[0, 0]$. Of course, this can only be possible for short sequences because the matrixes produced by long sequences will prove a great challenge for performing a visual traceback for an optimal solution.

The arrows and numbers shown in each cell were produced via repeated calls to the Java Graphics methods draw() and others to render the images of the following:

1. The matrix itself which is rendered as a 2-dimensional array for the LCS problem.
2. The cells within the matrix which are rendered as boxes with each one related to the boxes surrounding it within the matrix.
3. The numbers were then rendered to indicate the specific solution for that cell using the algorithm used to solve the cell and the matrix, and
4. The arrows were finally drawn based on the algorithm – match or mismatch – that produced the solution to that cell, whether pointing to the sequence on the vertical, or the sequence on the horizontal, or pointing to the diagonal in the direction of the matrix's origin.

This rendering of the matrix array, cells within the array, arrows, and numbers in the cells produced a complete picture of a real-life dynamic programming matrix. When completed, an array of possibilities of deducing the optimal solution, in this case the LCS between the 2 sequences, are immediately available and visible to the user.

I also computed the *edit distance* of the LCS alignment. The edit distance is the minimum cost of converting one sequence, the first one, S1, into the other one, S2, through insertions, deletions or replacements. It is a measure of the similarity between the 2 given sequences. (Dasgupta *et al.*, Chap.6)

RESULTS

DPMax for LCS creates a 2-dimensional LCS matrix, an array-of-arrays, comprising of cells of $Z[A_i, B_j]$, given 2 sequences, A and B, and displays same matrix for the user on a graphical user interface (GUI). Sequence A is the first sequence (S1) and it is always on the vertical and it represents the rows of the matrix. B is the second sequence (S2) and is aligned on the horizontal to represent the columns of the matrix. The length of S1 is N. However, because of the base relation of the LCS algorithm that adds an extra row and column at the start of the matrix, the number of rows, nRows, is N + 1. Likewise, while the length of S2 is M, the number of columns, nCols, is M + 1. There were three sets of experiments done with the finished version of DPMax – one was a pair of nucleotides and two sets were pairs of peptides. For the sake of brevity and conciseness, the set of shorter of peptides has been presented in the body of the paper. The results of the other two are located in the Appendices.

The Results for Two Peptide Sequences

The LCS between 2 short peptide sequences "APCDGHE" and "AEDFHRV" was determined. The output of results was displayed in text format on the 'Output' tab and the graphical display was presented on the 'Graphics' tab.

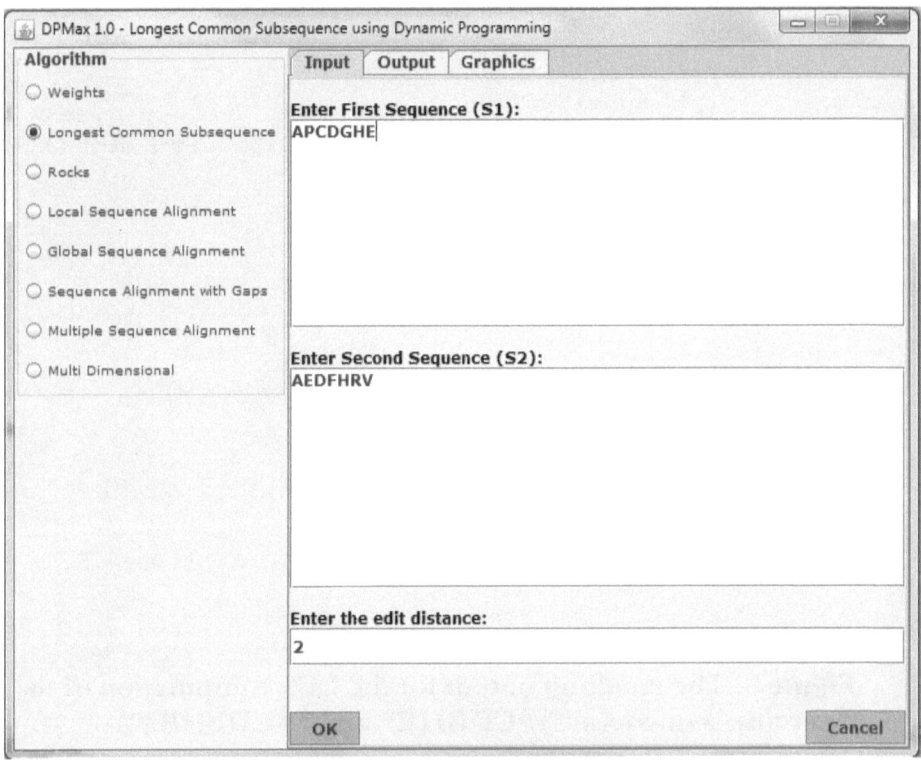

Figure 2: The Input tab display for DPMax for LCS

The first sequence is shown in the upper textbox and is designated S1. This is the sequence that will appear on the vertical (Y) axis of the LCS matrix. The second textbox is beneath the first one and it accepts as input the second sequence, S2, which will appear on the horizontal (X) axis of the matrix. The edit distance defaults to 2 but the algorithm will compute the actual edit distance as it computes the LCS. If the edit distance changes, the new edit distance from the LCS found will be displayed on the output tab.

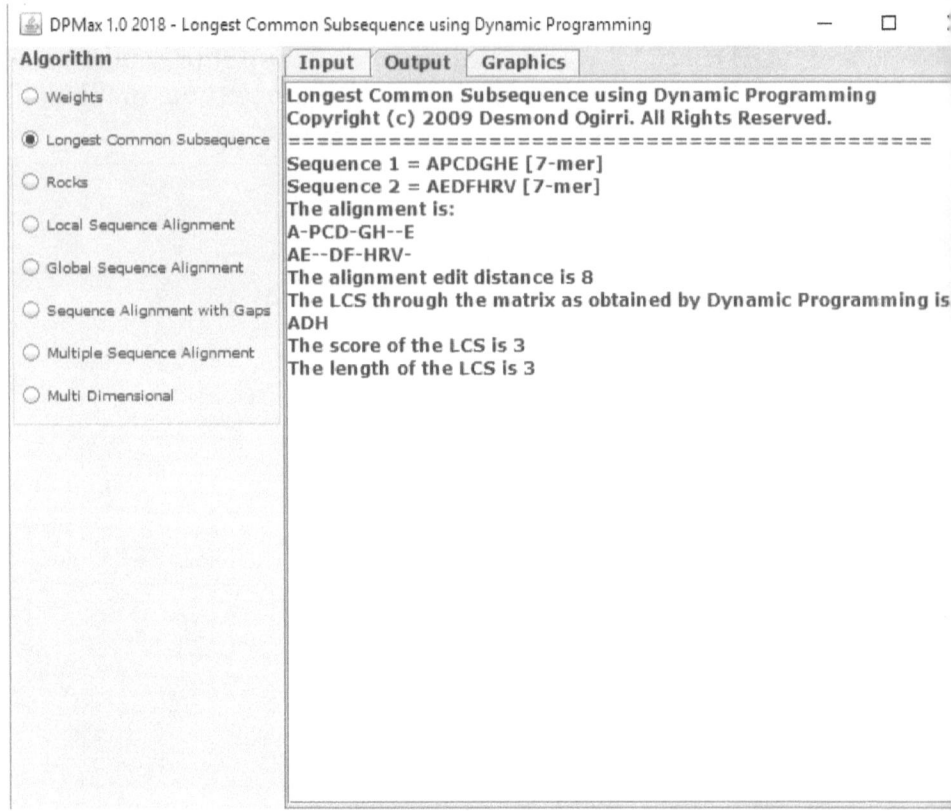

Figure 3: The resulting output for the LCS computation of the 2 peptide sequences "APCDGHE" and "AEDFHRV"

The output tab displays the results of the computation of the LCS between the 2 peptide sequences: "APCDGHE" and "AEDFHRV." It shows the LCS alignment of the 2 peptides and displays the actual LCS, the actual alignment edit distance, and the score (i.e. the length) of the LCS. The LCS alignment with an edit distance of 8 and score of 3 is shown in the next table.

A	-	P	C	D	-	G	H	-	-	E
A	E	-	-	D	F	-	H	R	V	-

Table 1: The LCS alignment of peptide sequences "APCDGHE" and "AEDFHRV"

On the next tab, which is the LCS 'Graphics' display tab, the results displayed on this tab will be explained from that perspective. These results will then be better understood.

The matches represent the similarity between the characters of the sequences while the mismatches represent the dissimilarity between the sequences. The gaps represent the characters where operations called 'indels' occur. This term simply represents the combination of insertions and deletions that need to occur to convert one sequence to the other one to make them similar. The gaps in S1, the first sequence, are the characters where insertions of the characters in the opposing sequence are needed to convert it into S2. And the gaps in S2 are the characters that need to be deleted to achieve the conversion. In other words, you are inserting in S1 and deleting in S2. In the result of the output of the alignment above, to transform S1 to S2, the characters 'EFRV' should be inserted while the characters 'PCGE' should be deleted.

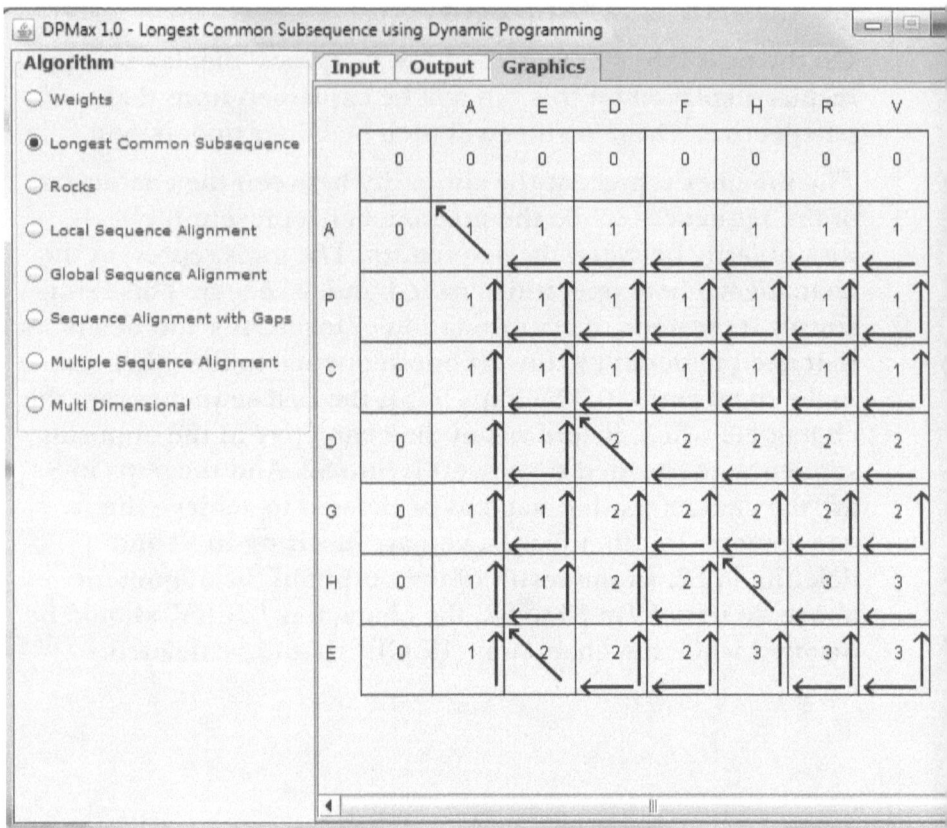

Figure 4: The 'Graphics' tab showing the graphical display of the results of the LCS alignment between the 2 peptide sequences: "APCDGHE" and "AEDFHRV"

One of the reasons of producing a graphical LCS display is to have a much more informed view of what the algorithm is doing and the solutions to the LCS itself. From the textual output we can see that the LCS score is 3, and this can at once be ascertained by one glance at the matrix. The optimal score of the alignment is found at the cell at $Z[nRows-1, nCols-1]$ or $Z[N, M]$. This is expected as this is an application of the bottom-up approach and it is where the largest or maximum sub-problem lies. This cell contains the optimal solution to the problem. The algorithm iterates through the matrix from top-to-bottom and left-to-right, solving each overlapping sub-problem as it goes. In this case the runtime is $O(N^2)$ because

$N = M = 7$. The optimal cell here is at $Z[A_7, B_7]$ with a global optimal score of 3.

A careful examination of the LCS alignment shows that the edit distance is 8. This is the sum of all the gaps found in both LCS alignments of the 2 sequences. There are 4 gaps in each of the resulting alignments. It also reveals that the matrix follows the algorithm by setting all the cells of the matrix to 0 in the first column and first row, since if $(j = 0)$, $Z[A_i, 0] = 0$, and if $(i = 0)$, $Z[0, B_j] = 0$.

At $Z[A_1, B_1]$, we have a cell that has a match of characters between the 2 sequences. The match of the amino acid 'A' (Alanine) means that the second part of the algorithm is applied. DPMax goes into the cell in the upper-left diagonal of the matching cell, which happens to be $Z[A_0, B_0]$ with a score of 0. The program increments the score by 1 and makes that the score of the matching cell whose score now becomes 1.

At the last cell of the matrix, $Z[N, M]$, we have a mismatch and the last scenario in the LCS algorithm is encountered. There is a mismatch between the 2 sequences at [S1=E, S2=V]. As in all other cases of a mismatch in the matrix, the maximum of the scores in both the upper cell at $Z[A_{i-1}, B_j]$ and the left cell at position $Z[A_i, B_{j-1}]$, is calculated. This value becomes the new score for this last cell of the matrix. And in this case, it is also the optimal value, or score, for our matrix and alignment.

The arrows in each cell represent one of the biggest pros of the program. A visual examination of the matrix showing the arrows at once reveals the numerous possibilities of alignments between the 2 sequences. It also shows the path or paths that were taken to solve each cell in the matrix. In other words, each arrow in a cell points to the cell from whence the solution for that cell was derived. For instance, the optimal cell has 2 arrows: one pointing to the cell above and the other one pointing to the cell to the left. This means that both cells, upper and left cells, both produced the solutions to the optimal cell. This shows that both cells which had scores of 3 could be a pathway to the optimal cell and therefore could each form alternative alignments when those alignments are computed. It must be noted that alignments can only be achieved along the pathway of arrows. So, if there is no arrow connecting one cell to another, then there is no alignment between the 2 sequences. Hence, an alternate pathway must be found which has an arrow connecting the 2 cells. It must also be noted that a traceback, whether visual or computational, is the only way to produce an LCS alignment, and hence an LCS. And, it must also be understood that the traceback must be done from the optimal cell leftward and upward through the matrix, and along the connecting arrows, until it ends at the very first cell.

This fact that multiple cells can produce solutions to any equal or larger cell, and therefore solutions to sub-problems, can be invaluable. This alignment may involve short peptides and a relatively common algorithm like the LCS, but this could be an LCS with much longer sequences, even up to hundreds of sequences. In such a case, every alternative alignment may be crucial to solving the problem at hand. Besides, the DP algorithm could be something very complicated or uncommon such that every resulting alignment from the multiple alignments found may be the difference between success and failure in a given project. One such DP algorithm could be the search for therapeutic peptides or sequences, whether peptide or nucleotide, with great biological or industrial value.

An examination of the arrows in the graphical display could be used to derive one or more alignments and LCS sequences. In this case, we know that the LCS can never be longer than 3 characters and the length of all the characters of any computed LCS string shouldn't be longer than 3. All LCS characters in any given LCS string can only be found at diagonal cells because this is where the character-matches between both sequences always occur in the matrix.

So, without any further coding to compute the LCS, we can deduce it from the graphical display, which in this case, it is the only one produced by the DPMax traceback function. It is the sequence, 'ADH,' which is derived from the matched characters of the cells at $Z[A_1, B_1]$, $Z[A_4, B_3]$, and $Z[A_6, B_5]$, respectively.

Again, the optimal solution is obtained in the cell at position $Z[A_N, B_M]$ ($Z[nRows_{-1}, nCols_{-1}]$). Traceback runs backwards from $Z[N, M]$ to $Z[1, 1]$.

Architecture, High-level Design and Program Flow

The whole of DPMax was built using the highly efficient object-oriented programming (OOP) paradigm and one of its signature architectural designs called 'MVC.' This is an acronym that stands for *Model-View-Controller* and it works quite simply. It is a 3-part architecture where the high-level control of the program is embedded within a component called a *Controller*. This class contains all the main components of the program and it delegates functionality to the other parts of the program as needed. The Model is where all data resources and functionality are obtained, kept and used. In all cases, the data produced during the computation of the algorithm's solution is transferred to the View class, or classes, for the viewing of the program's output by the user. The View classes present the graphical user interfaces (GUI) through which the user interacts with each module of the program.

All the different classes that contain the different functions of the various DP modules are contained in the Controller. The Controller employs another unique design pattern called the *Delegate*, among many others, to pass control to the different specific module controllers as necessary. These mini-Controller classes that contain the functionality for a given module will now handle the respective tasks for its own module such as Weights, LCS, Rocks, etc.

Every module has its classes and resources to handle its own unique algorithm, after which it will display the results from its Model classes on the View classes for the user to see. These View classes are simply Java panels on which the drawing of the various matrixes, or whatever final graphical presentation, have been performed. In the LCS, for instance, the View classes of the Graphical tab present a final JPanel on which the 2-dimensional matrix solution has been drawn.

The Main Controller - DPMaxController

public class DPMaxController extends JApplet implements ActionListener

DPMaxController is an applet that implements the interface ActionListener, listening and responding to all the actions performed by the user. It is responsible for building the main GUI panels on the left and right of the main GUI. It then builds each of the view panels by creating methods that creates each one of those views using the respective view class.

DynProgLCS is the class that has the code to create the GUI for the LCS function and also creates the functionality that handles the LCS algorithm itself.

The option panel (added to the left panel) is built in the DPMaxController to provide to the user to click on one of the many functionalities of the application. Once a user clicks one of the radio buttons on the option panel, it triggers the actionPerformed() methods of the Controller. This action causes the app to display the panel that contains the functionality of the button that was clicked. For instance, if the user clicks the '*Longest Common Subsequence*' radio button, the app displays the LCS module on the right main panel.

There are different Model and View classes. The View classes typically have the words Panel suffixed to their names. Examples of DPMax View classes include LCSDrawPanel, WeightsDrawPanel, etc. The Model or their helper utility classes typically have explanatory names like Cell, LCSCell, Constant, etc. some of these classes represent the mini-controller classes referred to previously.

The Typical Programmatic Flow

The program flow in the DPMax software is outlined below.

1. Controller makes a call to the diff view classes to build the two main panels – the main DPMax view display panel and then the GUI for accessing the various DP module panels.
2. The different view panels then present the functionality for their respective DP modules – LCS or Weights, etc.
3. 'Weights' is the first module while LCS is the second module and Rocks the third and so on. The LCS module is in focus in this paper.
4. Once they have received control, the various DP modules will carry out their own respective functionalities.

The Program Flow in the LCS View Panel/GUI

1. On the LCS panel, there are 3 possible GUI interactions – A) Input: For the input of the 2 sequences to be LCS-aligned. B) Output: For the display of the result of the alignment of the 2 sequences in text format, and, C) Graphics panel: is the display of the result of the alignment in graphic format which displays the LCS matrix built using DP.
2. Clicking on the button 'OK' on the input page calls the actionPerformed() method of the LCS View which hands control to the class DynProgLCS

The *DPMax for LCS* Module

The LCS Methods and Functions

The main class that contains the LCS module view and functionality is the DynProgLCS class. The *dpg* object encapsulates the functionality of the DPGraphics class.

The Input tab has an 'OK' button which when pressed triggers an action event that is sent to the actionPerformed() method in this class. Once in this method, the class reads the 2 sequences with Sequence 1 (S1 of length N) on the vertical and Sequence 2 (S2 with length M) on the horizontal. It stores the values for those strings in 2 class variables which are visible to all members and methods of the class. Once it does that, it calls the method doLCS() which reads the length of the 2 sequences and creates the 2-dimensional *M by N* LCS matrix based on those sequences. The matrix itself is a collection of objects of type LCSCell as encapsulated within that class. This means that each cell in the matrix is of type LCSCell.

Initializing the matrix scores

The doLCS() method then calls the method initialize() to initialize the matrix and it does so by creating each cell (which is created with an initial score of 0) and positioning them in the matrix. The initialize() method promptly calls helper method initializeScores() which will set the scores for each cell in that matrix based on the LCS algorithm base case and its cell-filling matrix numbers. The runtime for each of the calls to initialize the cell scores is $O(m)$ for S1 on the rows and $O(n)$ for S2 in the columns.

Filling the LCS Matrix: fillMatrix()

Once the initial scores have been fixed in each cell in the matrix, doLCS() then calls another method fillMatrix() to actually fill the matrix with the solution of each cell until it reaches the optimal solution. It is important to note here that my implementation of the LCS dynamic programming matrix is a bottom-up approach and not top-down. It starts by solving the cells which are the least problems and then uses the solutions for those cells that have been solved to find the solution for the overlapping cells which are bigger problems. It progresses upwards by solving the cells at the bottom of the matrix tree and builds upwards until it solves the biggest problems and then ends by solving the last cell which is the optimal solution. There is no need for recursion as in the top-down approach.

This method, which is responsible for filling the matrix of subproblems, implements the high-level routines of the LCS recurrence algorithm. It begins by going into a set of *for* loops and this is where the bulk of the runtime occurs. The first loop iterates over the characters of S1. The second, inner loop which runs immediately after the first one, iterates over the characters of S2. Within this code, the O(nm) runtime of the LCS algorithm occurs. The basic operation of solving each subproblem is done by the helper method that is called within this fillMatrix() method. That method, fillCell(), performs basic operations in constant $O(1)$ time.

By the end of fillMatrix(), each cell of the matrix has been given a solution score and the final optimal cell has been produced. fillMatrix() delegates its functionality to another method fillCell() to do the actual cell filling. fillCell() is an overloaded helper method which fills cells of the matrix by the LCS algorithm being used. After being filled, every cell is then connected to the surrounding cells round about, whether it's above, below, left, right or diagonal. Every cell must know its relative cells in the optimal substructure of Z.

Filling each cell: The fillCell() method

The function of the fillCell() method is quite straightforward. It is an overloaded method which takes as parameter either 3 or 4 different LCS cells. It takes 3 parameters – the current cell, the cell above and the cell to the left of the current cell – whenever there is a mismatch in the sequence characters. Otherwise, when there is a match, it takes 4 parameters – the three parameters as previously, and a fourth parameter – the cell in the upper left diagonal.

With these parameters, it builds connections and pointers between the cells as needed. It connects each cell to its surrounding cell and creates pointers that indicate which cell or cells provided the solution to the current cell. Every cell has pointers set to indicate where its solution came from and every cell also contains a class member which is an instance of java.util.Map where it stores all its connections to, and information about, its surrounding cells.

Once the matrix has been filled, we know its optimal solution. But the task is far from completed. We still need to find the actual sequence that makes up the optimal sequence that ends in the optimal solution. This is the final step in many dynamic programming modules and for the Longest Common subsequence, it is what gives us the actual sequence that we have been searching for – the *LCS* between S1 and S2. All this is done through something called a *traceback* – a technique for finding the final solution of our LCS matrix that contains the optimal solution so found. It is aptly called a traceback because it does exactly what its name implies – it walks backwards through the matrix starting at the optimal solution down to the beginning of the matrix. This code obtains its LCS through the doTraceback() function that returns the LCS as a String object. The purpose of the traceback is to build the optimal LCS alignment. Once the alignment is attained, the LCS will be the sequence of characters that match in the alignments of both sequences.

This traceback is a simple version of a typical traceback. It takes the matrix and all its cells and starts from the cell with the optimal solution. This cell is at $Z[A_N][B_M]$ and it traces back all the cells that led up to the optimal solution. At the start of the traceback, the optimal cell is the current cell but that would change throughout the traceback. At each stage of the traceback, cell by cell, you can either have a match or a mismatch. Let's call the new alignment sequences S3 (based on the alignment of S1) and S4 (based on the alignment of S2). If the cell that provided the solution to the current cell is above the current cell, it adds the character from S2 to the new alignment sequence S4. Otherwise, a gap ('-') is added to S4. S3 and S4 are represented by the class StringBuffers *buf1* and *buf2* respectively. Local method variable StringBuffer *lcs2* builds the actual LCS and returns it as a String object.

Likewise, if the cell to the left of the optimal cell was the solution that led to the current cell, then the character of S1 at that cell is added to S3. Otherwise, a gap ('-') is added at that position in S3. Notice that the new alignment sequences are built from right to left in the order the traceback walks through the cells of the matrix. If the cell in the diagonal of the current cell is the cell that was the solution to the current cell, then both S3 and S4 have the same matching characters from the original sequences S1 and S2. There are no gaps in either alignment sequences. At the end of this assignment the solution cell that led to the current cell – whether it is left, above or diagonal – is now assigned to the current cell and the loop continues. This loop goes on until there are no more cells in the matrix to trace back.

Throughout the traceback, the code also computes the alignment edit distance.

Once the traceback is completed, the matches between the S3 and S4 are obtained as the *longest common subsequence* between the original sequences S1 and S2.

```
public static void doLCS() {
        nRows = strSeq1.trim().length() + 1;
        nCols = strSeq2.trim().length() + 1;
        int seq1Len = strSeq1.trim().length();
        int seq2Len = strSeq2.trim().length();
```

```java
            lcsLen = getLCSLength(nRows, nCols, editDist);
            matrix = new LCSCell[nRows][nCols];

            //now compute the scores and all else
            initialize();
            fillMatrix();

            String output1 = "The LCS through the matrix as obtained by " +
                            "Dynamic Programming is...\n";
            String lcs = doTraceback();
            String seq1 = "Sequence 1 = " + strSeq1 + " [" + seq1Len + "-mer]";
            String seq2 = "Sequence 2 = " + strSeq2 + " [" + seq2Len + "-mer]";
            String ruler = "\n================================================\n";
            String align = "The alignment is:\n" + buf1 +
                            "\n" + buf2 + "\n" +
                            "The alignment edit distance is " + alignEdDist + "\n";

            if (lcs.length() <= lcsLen){
                lcsLen = lcs.length();
            }else{
                lcs = lcs.substring(0, lcsLen);
            }
            String output2 = "\nThe score of the LCS is " + score +
                            "\nThe length of the LCS is " + lcsLen;
            txtArea3.append(ruler +
                            seq1 + "\n" + seq2 + "\n" +
            align + output1 + lcs + output2);
```

```
        //draw the matrix
        dpg.setLcsMatrix(matrix);
        dpg.setStrSeq1(strSeq1);
        dpg.setStrSeq2(strSeq2);

    }
```

```java
public static int getLCSLength (int seq1Len, int seq2Len, int editDist){
    int lcsLen = ( (seq1Len + seq2Len - editDist) / 2 );
    return lcsLen;
}

public static void initialize() {
    //get the weights that we need for the whole table
    for (int row = 0; row < nRows; row++) {
        for (int col = 0; col < nCols; col++)
        {
            matrix[row][col] = new LCSCell(row, col);
        }
    }
    initializeScores();
}

public static void initializeScores(){
    int score = 0;

    //set the scores for each cell
    //at first column ie column 0 and row row
    //at the first column the prev cell is the cell above
    //except for the first cell at 0, 0
    for (int row = 0; row < nRows; row++) {
        matrix[row][0].setScore(score);
        if (row != 0){
            LCSCell prevCell = matrix[row-1][0];
            char seq1Char = strSeq1.charAt(row-1);

            matrix[row][0].setPrevCell(prevCell);

            matrix[row][0].setSeq1Char(seq1Char);
```

```java
            }
        }

        //then set the scores for each cell
        //at first row ie column col and row 0
        //at the first row the prev cell is the cell to the
        //left except for the first cell at 0, 0
        for(int col = 0; col < nCols; col++){
            matrix[0][col].setScore(score);
            if (col != 0) {
                LCSCell prevCell = matrix[0][col-1];

                char seq2Char = strSeq2.charAt(col-1);

                matrix[0][col].setPrevCell(prevCell);

                matrix[0][col].setSeq2Char(seq2Char);
            }
        }
    }

    //The rule for filling the LCS matrix is:
    //1. if Ai == Bj (meaning we have a match between the 2 sequences)
    //the score for the cell is max of either the diagonal OR the left OR
    //the right cells
    //2. otherwise (we don't have a match) and then
    // the score of the current cell is the max of either the left OR right cells
    public static void fillMatrix() {
        for (int row = 1; row < nRows; row++) {
            for (int col = 1; col < nCols; col++) {
                LCSCell currentCell = matrix[row][col];
                LCSCell cellAbove = matrix[row - 1][col];
                LCSCell cellToLeft = matrix[row][col - 1];
                LCSCell cellInDiag = matrix[row - 1][col - 1];
```

```java
            if(strSeq1.charAt(row-1) != strSeq2.charAt(col-1)){
               fillCell(currentCell, cellAbove, cellToLeft);
            }else{
               fillCell(currentCell, cellAbove, cellToLeft, cellInDiag);
            }
            currentCell.setSeq1Char(strSeq1.charAt(row-1));
            currentCell.setSeq2Char(strSeq2.charAt(col-1));
          }
        }
      }


      public static void fillCell (LCSCell currentCell, LCSCell cellAbove,
                    LCSCell cellToLeft) {
            int aboveScore = cellAbove.getScore();
            int leftScore = cellToLeft.getScore();

            int cellScore = 0;
            LCSCell prevCell;
            Map<String, LCSCell> pcMap = new HashMap<String, LCSCell>();
            if (leftScore >= aboveScore) {
              if (leftScore > aboveScore) {
                cellScore = leftScore;
                prevCell = cellToLeft;
                pcMap.put(Constant.CELL_TO_LEFT, cellToLeft);
              } else {
                  //ideally if they are the same the two
                  //should both be set as pointers
                  // leftScore == aboveScore
                  cellScore = aboveScore;
                  prevCell = cellAbove;
                  pcMap.put(Constant.CELL_TO_LEFT, cellToLeft);
                  pcMap.put(Constant.CELL_ABOVE, cellAbove);
```

```
                    }
                } else {//aboveScore > leftScore

                    cellScore = aboveScore;
                    prevCell = cellAbove;
                    pcMap.put(Constant.CELL_ABOVE, cellAbove);
                }
                currentCell.setScore(cellScore);
                currentCell.setPrevCell(prevCell);
                currentCell.setPrevCellMap(pcMap);
    }


        public static void fillCell(LCSCell currentCell, LCSCell cellAbove,
                    LCSCell cellToLeft, LCSCell cellInDiag) {
                int aboveScore = cellAbove.getScore();
                int leftScore = cellToLeft.getScore();
                int diagScore = cellInDiag.getScore() + 1;

                int cellScore = 0;
                LCSCell prevCell;
                LCSCell cellAbove2 = null;
                LCSCell cellToLeft2 = null;
                LCSCell cellInDiag2 = null;
                Map<String, LCSCell> pcMap = new HashMap<String, LCSCell>();
                //As in the fillCell method with only 2 possible
                //previous cells above, there should be a list/array of
                //previous cells. so that every cell can have all possible
                //previous cells set. this will enable the matrix to produce
                //all possible paths/LCS candidates
                if (diagScore >= aboveScore) {
                    if(diagScore > aboveScore){
```

```
                        if (diagScore >= leftScore) {
                            if (diagScore > leftScore) {
                                //diagScore > aboveScore and diagScore > leftScore
                                cellScore = diagScore;
                                prevCell = cellInDiag;
                                cellInDiag2 = cellInDiag;
                                pcMap.put(Constant.CELL_IN_DIAG, cellInDiag);
                            }else {
                                // diagScore > aboveScore and diagScore == leftScore
                                cellScore = diagScore;
                                prevCell = cellInDiag;
                                cellInDiag2 = cellInDiag;
                                pcMap.put(Constant.CELL_IN_DIAG, cellInDiag);
                                pcMap.put(Constant.CELL_TO_LEFT, cellToLeft);
                            }
                        } else {
                            // leftScore > diagScore > aboveScore
                            cellScore = leftScore;
                            prevCell = cellToLeft;
                            cellToLeft2 = cellToLeft;
                            pcMap.put(Constant.CELL_TO_LEFT, cellToLeft);
                        }
                    }else{
                        //diagScore == aboveScore
                        //default is diagonal
                        cellScore = diagScore;
                        prevCell = cellInDiag;
                        cellInDiag2 = cellInDiag;
                        pcMap.put(Constant.CELL_IN_DIAG, cellInDiag);
                        pcMap.put(Constant.CELL_ABOVE, cellAbove);
```

```
                        }
                } else {
                        //aboveScore > diagScore
                    if (aboveScore >= leftScore) {
                        if (aboveScore > leftScore) {
                            // aboveScore > diagScore
and aboveScore > leftScore
                            cellScore = aboveScore;
                            prevCell = cellAbove;
                            cellAbove2 = cellAbove;

pcMap.put(Constant.CELL_ABOVE, cellAbove);
                        }else{
                            // aboveScore >
diagScore and aboveScore == leftScore
                            //default prev cell is
above cell
                            cellScore = aboveScore;
                            prevCell = cellAbove;
                            cellAbove2 = cellAbove;
                            cellToLeft2 = cellToLeft;

pcMap.put(Constant.CELL_ABOVE, cellAbove);

pcMap.put(Constant.CELL_TO_LEFT, cellToLeft);
                        }
                    } else {
                        // leftScore > aboveScore >
diagScore
                        cellScore = leftScore;
                        prevCell = cellToLeft;
                        cellToLeft2 = cellToLeft;

pcMap.put(Constant.CELL_TO_LEFT, cellToLeft);
                    }
                }
            currentCell.setScore(cellScore);
            currentCell.setPrevCell(prevCell);
            currentCell.setCellAbove(cellAbove2);
            currentCell.setCellInDiag(cellInDiag2);
```

```
            currentCell.setCellToLeft(cellToLeft2);
            currentCell.setPrevCellMap(pcMap);
}
```

The Graphical output

The graphical output was also created within the same doLCS() function that created the functionality of the non-graphical output. The graphical functionality is encapsulated within the DPGraphics class which serves as both a panel and event listener that does the high-level event listening and actions and contains the main drawing panel. It receives the user interaction from the container app deals with those action or mouse events. This DPGraphics class delegates the heavy lifting drawing to another panel, the main drawing panel called LCSDrawPanel. It is this class that contains all the drawing capabilities that display the graphical LCS matrix. It does most of its drawing in a method called drawMatrix() which takes as input parameters, an LCSCell matrix and the 2 input string sequences upon which to perform LCS.

Whenever the Java Graphics system displays a JPanel object, it makes a call to the class's method paintComponent(), passing it the system's java.awt.Graphics object as a parameter. The LCSDrawPanel uses this Graphics object and renders the matrix object as an array of arrays of LCSCell objects. Each cell is created and drawn with its score in the center of the cell. In each cell there is an arrow/arrows in each cell that point/points to the cell from where its own solution was derived. For instance, in the cell with the optimal solution, if the only solution was derived from the cell in the diagonal, then there would be an arrow pointing to the diagonal and not to the left nor above. If the cells in both the left (S1) and top (S2) sequences respectively were solutions to the optimal cell, there would be arrows pointing above and to the left.

paintComponent() can also be called explicitly by the repaint() method also in the JPanel and this would redraw the whole matrix in case there's been a change in the Input tab and new sequences have been submitted. The scroller() method is called to display a scroller if necessary and the repaint() method is called at the end of the scroller() to redraw the matrix.

The main function for drawing the matrix: drawMatrix(...)

```java
public void drawMatrix(LCSCell[][] matrix, String strSeq1,
                String strSeq2)
{
            if (matrix == null || strSeq1 == null || strSeq2 == null)
                    return;
            int x = 30;
            int y = 30;
            int x1 = 0;
            int x2 = 0;
            int y1 = 0;
            int y2 = 0;
            int x3 = 0;
            int y3 = 0;
            int width = 50;
            int height = 50;
            int row;
            int col;
            String score;
            Stroke prevStk;
            Stroke boldStk = new BasicStroke(2f);
            String seq = "";
            Map<String, LCSCell> prevCellMap = null;
            area = new Dimension();
            g2d = (Graphics2D)gr;
        for (row = 0; row < matrix.length; row++) {

            // y += 50;
                for (col = 0; col < matrix[0].length; col++) {

                    LCSCell currentCell = matrix[row][col];
                    LCSCell prevCell = currentCell.getPrevCell();
                    prevCellMap = currentCell.getPrevCellMap();
```

```
                        //if the prev cell is null just draw
the current cell
                   if (prevCell == null)
                   {
                       g2d.drawRect(x, y, width, height);
                   }
                   else //draw the currentcell and get the
direction of the
                       //prevcell so we can draw arrows
pointing to it
                       //and then draw the score and the
sequence chars
                       //
                   {
                       g2d.drawRect(x, y, width, height);
                       prevStk = g2d.getStroke();
                       //if(prevCell.isCellAbove(currentCell)){

if(prevCellMap.get(Constant.CELL_ABOVE) != null) {
                            x1 = x + width;
                            y1 = y + 7;
                            x2 = x1;
                            y2 = y + height - 7;
                            x1 = x1 - 5;
                            x2 = x2 - 5;
                            if(row != 0 && col != 0)
                            {
                                    g2d.setStroke(boldStk);
                                    g2d.drawLine(x1, y1, x2,
y2);
                                    //now draw the arrows
                                    x2 = x1 - 5;
                                    y2 = y1 + 5;
                                    x3 = x1 + 5;
                                    y3 = y1 + 5;
                                    g2d.drawLine(x1, y1, x2,
y2);
                                    g2d.drawLine(x1, y1, x3,
y3);
                                    g2d.setStroke(prevStk);
```

```
            }
        }

    if(prevCellMap.get(Constant.CELL_TO_LEFT) != null) {
                    x1 = x + 10;
                    y1 = y + height - 5;
                    x2 = x + width - 5;
                    y2 = y1 ;
                    x1 = x1 - 5;
                    x2 = x2 - 5;
                    if(row != 0 && col != 0)
                    {

g2d.setStroke(boldStk);

g2d.drawLine(x1, y1, x2, y2);
                                        //now draw
the arrows
                    x2 = x1 + 5;
                    y2 = y1 - 5;
                    x3 = x1 + 5;
                    y3 = y1 + 5;

g2d.drawLine(x1, y1, x2, y2);

g2d.drawLine(x1, y1, x3, y3);

g2d.setStroke(prevStk);
                    }
                }
            //
if(prevCell.isCellInDiag(currentCell)){

        if(prevCellMap.get(Constant.CELL_IN_DIAG) !=
null) {
                    x1 = x + 10;
                    y1 = y + 5;
```

```
                              x2 = x + width - 5;
                              y2 = y + height - 10;
                              x1 = x1 - 5;
                              x2 = x2 - 5;
                              if(row != 0 && col != 0)
                              {

g2d.setStroke(boldStk);

g2d.drawLine(x1, y1, x2, y2);
                                           //now draw
the arrows
                              x2 = x1 ;
                              y2 = y1 + 5;
                              x3 = x1 + 5;
                              y3 = y1;

g2d.drawLine(x1, y1, x2, y2);

g2d.drawLine(x1, y1, x3, y3);

g2d.setStroke(prevStk);
                                          }

                             }
                           }


                           //now draw the score
                           score = String.valueOf(
currentCell.getScore() );
                           x1 = x + (width/2);
                           y1 = y + (height/2);
                           g2d.drawString(score, x1, y1);

                           x += 50;

                           if(col != 0){
                              if(row == 0){
```

```
                              seq = String.valueOf(
strSeq2.charAt(col-1) );
                              x1 = x - (width/2);
                              y1 = y - (height/4);
                              g2d.drawString(seq, x1, y1);
                    }
                  }


                }
                if (row == 0)
                  area.width += x;

                  x = 30;
                  y += 50;

                if(row != 0){
                        seq = String.valueOf(
strSeq1.charAt(row-1) );
                        x1 = x - (width/2);
                        y1 = y - (height/2);
                         g2d.drawString(seq, x1, y1);

                }
              }
        area.height = y;
      }
```

The Traceback function: doTraceback()

Now we shall look at the routines of the backtracking function known as the *traceback*. All the code for the traceback is contained in the method called doTraceback().

```
public static String doTraceback()
{
StringBuffer lcs = new StringBuffer();
StringBuffer lcs2 = new StringBuffer();
buf1 = new StringBuffer();
buf2 = new StringBuffer();
alignEdDist = 0;
LCSCell currentCell = matrix[nRows - 1][nCols - 1];
LCSCell prevCell;
score = currentCell.getScore();

while(currentCell.getPrevCell() != null){
        while(currentCell.getScore() >= 0){
        prevCell = currentCell.getPrevCell();

        if (prevCell.isCellAbove(currentCell)) {
                buf2.insert(0, currentCell.getSeq2Char());
        } else {
                buf2.insert(0, '-');
                alignEdDist++;
        }

        if (prevCell.isCellToLeft(currentCell)) {
                buf1.insert(0, currentCell.getSeq1Char());
        } else {
                buf1.insert(0, '-');
                alignEdDist++;
        }

        if (currentCell.charsMatch() &&
prevCell.isCellInDiag(currentCell))
        {
                lcs2.insert(0, currentCell.getSeq1Char());
        }
```

```
        currentCell = prevCell;
}
        for (int i = 0; i < buf1.length(); i++){
                if(buf1.charAt(i) == buf2.charAt(i)){
                        lcs.append(buf1.charAt(i));
                }
        }
        return lcs2.toString();
}
```

Analysis of the Traceback

Now we shall return and perform an analysis of the traceback method and its operations. Before I continue, I wish to make a very important point and distinction. There should be no confusion between the actual LCS and the LCS alignment. The LCS is the longest common subsequence between the 2 sequences. It is a single sequence of the matches between the 2 sequences. The LCS alignment is the alignment of the path of solutions from the beginning of the 2 sequences to the pair of characters in the optimal cell. It comprises of matches of characters and gaps where there are mismatches in the sequences' characters. These could be multiple LCS alignments, each of which must end at the characters, match or mismatch, of the optimal cell. Every LCS alignment must contain an LCS. All LCS alignments must clearly show the characters that make up the LCS – these are the only characters that will match between the 2 sequences.

This traceback method is a deceptively simple one for a few reasons. It simply iterates backwards through the matrix it built to solve the LCS. In this simplified version of a backtracking operation, the code regresses along a list of cells which are interconnected by being members of a path of one possible, or only, optimization solution. That is, each character, i, in the sequence is a solution to the character, $i+1$, in front of it. So, the optimal cell is the final solution and all that is needed is to regresses backwards along that path starting from the optimal cell. It follows then, that the time taken to traverse this list is simply $O(k)$, where k is the length of the cells of solutions from the cell at the beginning of this list to the optimal cell at the end.

A typical traceback, however, should cost much more in time. Assuming that S1 and S2 were both very short sequences, say about 5 to 7 long, then the traceback could actually be done by visual inspection on the graphical view. This is one of the reasons for adding a graphical output to the program, and indeed for building the program itself. If S1 and S2 are both 5 peptides long, then the user can simply look at the graphical display of the matrix and quickly, but carefully, construct an alignment and then the LCS.

But, in the real world there are hardly cases when the sequences are short. The original sequences are often much longer than 7 and may be in the order of hundreds of amino acids and nucleotides. In this case, visual inspection would be very hard talk less of building alignment sequences or LCS sequences by just using the graphical matrix. In such a case, there will be multiple LCS sequences. Even using the computer to calculate the number of such sequences would be daunting. Needless to say, the simple N x M traceback employed here would be very time-consuming and perhaps inefficient. A much more time-efficient algorithm has to be employed and the traceback may then consume a huge part of the time to find the numerous LCSes discovered.

DISCUSSION

DPMax set out to simplify the Weights and LCS processes and it has achieved its main goal with great results. From the results of LCS modules, we can infer that the various modules, when completed, will provide the following benefits.

1. Simplification of the DP solution for each module.
2. It enables the visualization of the DP algorithm in action.
3. Find without computation the matrix alignments at first glance.
4. Be able to apply more complex algorithms without the need to create a new matrix or new computation.
5. Provide a deeper understanding of the DP (LCS-DP, Weights-DP and others) process and comparison between the text and graphical results.
6. Keep paper records or digital copies of the results of the matrix for further analysis and future references.
7. Sharing the results with colleagues, the public or make official and public presentations using them.
8. Creating new solutions of algorithms using visual inspection by application of the results of existing matrixes.

If there is one point that DPMax has proven, it is that visualizing DP matrixes is by far more useful and productive than otherwise. Whether it be simple text printout of the result or manual plotting of the matrix, the computational production of the solution of any DP algorithm is always more beneficial. There are a few unique scenarios where DPMax applications can be of immense use. Future versions of the application would not only continue work on 2-dimensional matrixes like the one presented here but will also focus on multidimensional algorithms and the benefits that they may present. Needless to say, future versions of DPMax would be directed towards bioinformatics and biomedical applications.

Another goal was to show that dynamic programming is a key algorithmic technique in the computational-mathematical-statistical analyses of biomolecules. DP is the one technique that is commonly found in any area of bioinformatics regardless of the nature of the problems encountered in that specialty. Whether it is phylogeny, DNA or RNA analyses, proteomics or biological databases, the application of DP is ubiquitous.

It is these reasons, and others, that prompted the creation of software that attempts to aggregate some of the most basic algorithms that display the application of DP. Also, it is my hope that the creation of this software will teach the skills of DP and reinforce what is already known about the theory of the algorithmic technique. So, even though the project looks quite ambitious, its goals and intents are well justified.

Improvements and Future Versions

There are certain additions to the software that should be included in future versions of the software. These include some of the following:

1. Printing: The capability of any software to print its output or data is vital to the robustness of the program specifications and user convenience and acceptance. The DPMax software is no exception to this fact. In future versions, it will be able to print both its text and graphical outputs. This functionality will involve the manipulation of the drawing panel in the graphics tab, and the text areas in the text output tab, to print their contents. Since the information in the Input tab is always replicated in the text output tab, there will be no need to print the contents of the Input tab. The print of large graphical matrixes must be created to fit onto pages of paper while showing all the parts of the matrixes as produced in the application's graphical output.
2. Resizing of GUI: Maximizing the GUI to show the output results for large inputs is a necessary inclusion in future versions of DPMax. Some input sequences may be so large that their outputs would span a large space in the app's graphical output. A user should be able to enlarge the app in such a case to see as much of the matrix as possible. The software should be able to resize as necessary to fit the matrix, as large as it may be, into the Graphical panel to be viewed by the user. If the matrix is so large that it can't be viewed within the full computer screen, then vertical and horizontal scrollbars should be provided so that the user can view the full matrix by scrolling.
3. Multi-dimensional algorithms: The inclusion of DP algorithms that employ multi-dimensional matrixes

should be a priority in DPMax software upgrades. This topic will be covered in more detail later.
4. Storage in Permanent Datastores: It is always a big step-up for any software when it can write its output to a permanent record store like a database. DPMax data from the input, text output and the graphical output, including the matrix itself, can be written out to database or disk. This will enable the work done on the software to be retrieved and studied further at a later date. A connection to a database can be created in one or more Model classes while the SQL insert statements can be placed and accessed from resource files within the app's packages. The matrix can be obtained via serialization of the JPanel objects and converted into graphic picture formats, like PNG and JPG etc., and written out to database.
5. Correct Namespacing, Packaging and Object-Orientation: Inspection of the DPMax code would show that there is one main package (ogirri.dp) in which all classes reside. This can be modularized to contain different packages for each module. and then each module may have its different subpackages for the different classes of the MVC design pattern already discussed. For instance, the Weights module should be in its own distinct package, and it should have unique namespaces for View classes for displaying the graph containing the edges, and also for the Model classes that would create and manipulate the Weights data. The same design and namespacing should apply to the LCS and other modules in the DPMax software. Also, there should be a clear separation between the various MVC units especially the last two – model and view classes.
6. Scalability: Scalability is the ability to handle increasing amounts of input and output data and usage and still function correctly. The software should be made scalable by making it modular, able to write

large amounts of data to multiple datasources, extensive menu options and various look-and-feel themes. It could also be comprised of different modules that could be used as individual APIs for external programs, and so on. Most importantly is the use of algorithms and data structures that can handle any amounts of input and output data, large or small. For instance, the use of BigDecimals and BigIntegers rather than Doubles and Integers, where necessary.

7. Portability: DPMax should be made portable so that it is usable not only on desktops and laptops but also on mobile and online platforms. This could be solved by porting the code into web application format and applets for online platforms, and creating it as a mobile app for mobile devices. It should eventually be ported and scaled-up into a client-server architecture for the purpose of serving enterprise clients and corporate users.

8. AI and Deep Learning: One of the priorities in advancing this software is to integrate it with techniques of Artificial Intelligence and deep machine learning. This combination would empower it to intelligently find cures for diseases, find therapies for genetic mutations, and perform more advanced sequence analysis. For instance, the new intelligent DPMax could predict one or more tertiary or quaternary structures that may be the perfect cure for a particular disease condition. Indeed, future versions of this software would focus on AI-enabled drug discovery, therapeutic discovery, and complex analyses of biomolecular entities.

MULTI-DIMENSIONAL DP MATRIXES, BACKTRACKING AND OTHER ALGORITHMS

It is possible to have matrixes that span multiple dimensions so as to achieve the optimal solution for the given problem. In this case, the runtime of the matrix would be N^m, where m is the number of dimensions. This formula assumes that the lengths of all the sequences in the matrix are N. In reality, the real value for N should be

N = π (N-ary product) of i from 1 to 7, N_i

$$\prod_{i=0}^{N} x_i$$

For instance, if there are 7 different sequences then there are 7 dimensions of depth to explore and compute so as to find the global optimal solution between all 7 sequences. Needless to say, then that these 7 dimensions need no less than 7 internal loops and therefore will require a runtime of $O(N^7)$. There are a few points that need to be made to round off our discussion on the DPMax application.

1. It is possible to query N number of items or sequences by a DP-multidimensional matrix and obtain a solution in the cell at the last position of the matrix. It is then possible using the arrows to obtain the path of a particular solution using trace back from the final cell which is the global optimal solution. After achieving the desired path of the solution from the optimal position in the matrix through the matrix to the start of the matrix, a list can be made of such solutions.

2. An alternative solutions-gathering algorithm - a more computationally intensive but more robust one - would be to apply the full backtrack algorithm to derive this list of alignment-cum-solutions that are produced from the global

optimum cell of the matrix. This algorithm would find all the LCS alignments which are optimal solutions to the problem solved by the matrix. This version of the traceback could be quite intensive given the number of solutions produced by a matrix of significant size. The typical runtime of such a traceback would be exponential, and therefore quite costly computationally. So, the more the solutions, the greater the computational time required to derive a list of solutions. Given a multi-dimensional matrix, a traceback for even short sequences will certainly take quite a long time.

3. There is then the matter of the quality of solutions in the list of solutions produced by the backtrack algorithm. Though it is true that we now have solutions, but in the case of tens, thousands or even millions of solutions, how do we tell between the better solutions since the optimal score is the same for all of them. Some solutions make be of greater quality than others, while some may be almost useless in our specific search, whatever it may be. Let us suppose that our search is for the all-important cure for a disease. In this case, only the best of the reported solutions will do.

4. An elegant method to find the best of the optimal solutions may be to apply a simple scoring function to discover the quality of each solution and separate the best from all the others. This scoring function could be a classifier and would have the sole purpose of producing the very best from the list of solutions. A good scoring function would be the Bayesian Theorem which is a classification algorithm that reports the posterior hypothesis in the form of a conditional probability. Other classification methods may be applied to distinguish the individual solutions based on criteria like edit distance, the biochemical properties of the amino acids or nucleotides in each sequence and their primary and predicted secondary and tertiary structures.

5. The Bayesian Theorem reports the conditional probability of a model based on the data. It is a classification technique which gives us the ability – in the form of a probability – of each sequence or path to solve the particular problem at hand. This, in simple terms, means that the theorem will tell us the

probability, or score, of how well each solution will solve the problem. Using these scores, we can sort our list according to which one is/ones are best for solving the problem at hand. Of course, to apply the Bayesian function, we first have to obtain the various probabilities associated with each of our optimal solutions with respect to our given task.

6. One of the ways to generate probabilities needed for the classification of solutions is to compute the probabilities based on the purpose the solutions will serve. For instance, a set of LCS peptides that will be used for therapeutic purposes would have unique conditions that must be met for that purpose to be achieved. Each amino acid, with its unique chemical properties, will vary in its ability to solve a particular task. Also, particular RNA secondary structures vary in their abilities to produce a particular peptide structure or function. It is this unique set of conditions that will distinguish between the lesser, and the better solutions, and the best one.

7. Once we do that, we can proceed to find the optimal solution for that molecule with the greatest promise for curing that disease or producing that vaccine, or serving some other therapeutic purpose, or any other purpose for that matter.

Practical Applications of Longest Common Subsequences

1. One of the greatest applications of LCS is discovering, or inferring, similar functions or structures between peptides and proteins.

2. Finding any common evolutionary ancestry between nucleotides and peptides.

3. Discovering similarity in translation products of nucleotides.

4. Comparing the granularity of the functions between 2 or more similar peptides or nucleotides of related ancestry.

5. A good example of the uses of sequence comparison techniques, including LCS, for similarity searches is the discovery of the cystic fibrosis, CF, gene, and its function. Cystic fibrosis is a well-known mutation, which is caused by a

faulty mechanism in the gene. A search for the gene's function was narrowed to a region on Chromosome 7, which was compared via similarity searches to sequences in a database. The search matched a gene whose function was known and hence the function of the CF gene was inferred and is today well-known. The short story can be found in the *Algorithms* book by Dasgupta et. al. (Dasgupta, et. al., p. 148).

ACKNOWLEDGEMENT

1. All the faculty of Centennial College, and especially the faculty of the program *Bioinformatics for Software Professionals.*
2. And most especially, great thanks to Dr. M. Mbobi, who was my thesis advisor.

When I wrote version 1.0 of DPMax, I was a graduating graduate student at Centennial College and my name was Desmond Ogirri as the copyright on the software correctly states. But since then, my name has changed to Christian Colossus as the name on this paper states. I hope I have corrected any confusion or misunderstanding. Future versions of the software will make that correction.

CITATIONS

Baase, Sara, and Allen Van Gelder. *Computer Algorithms: Introduction to Design and Analysis.* 3rd ed., Addison-Wesley Longman, 2000.

Baxevanis, Andreas D., and B. F. Francis Ouellette, editors. *Bioinformatics: A Practical Guide to the Analysis of Genes and Proteins.* 3rd ed, Wiley, 2005.

Bellman, Richard, and Stuart Dreyfus. *Dynamic Programming.* 1. Princeton Landmarks in Mathematics ed., With a new introduction, Princeton University Press, 2010.

Bradley, Stephen P., et al. Applied Mathematical Programming. Addison-Wesley Pub. Co, 1977.

Chong, Jike, et al. *Dynamic Programming Pattern.* https://patterns.eecs.berkeley.edu/?page_id=416. Accessed Apr. 2009.

Cooper, Leon, and Mary W. Cooper. *Introduction to Dynamic Programming.* 1st ed, Pergamon Press, 1981.

Cormen, Thomas H., editor. *Introduction to Algorithms.* 3rd ed, MIT Press, 2009.

Dasgupta, Sanjoy, et. al. *Algorithms*. McGraw-Hill Higher Education, 2008.

Denardo, Eric V. *Dynamic Programming: Models and Applications*. Dover Publications, 2003.

GeeksforGeeks. *Overlapping Subproblems Property in Dynamic Programming | DP-1* https://www.geeksforgeeks.org/overlapping-subproblems-property-in-dynamic-programming-dp-1/. Accessed November 13, 2018.

Mount, David W. *Bioinformatics: Sequence and Genome Analysis*. 2nd ed, Cold Spring Harbor Laboratory Press, 2004.

Needleman, S. B., and C. D. Wunsch. "A General Method Applicable to the Search for Similarities in the Amino Acid Sequence of Two Proteins." *Journal of Molecular Biology*, vol. 48, no. 3, Mar. 1970, pp. 443–53.

Reingold, Edward M., et al. *Combinatorial Algorithms: Theory and Practice*. Prentice-Hall, 1977.

Smith, T. F., and M. S. Waterman. "Identification of Common Molecular Subsequences." *Journal of Molecular Biology*, vol. 147, no. 1, Mar. 1981, pp. 195–97.

Skiena, Steven S. *The Algorithm Design Manual.* 2nd ed, Springer, 2010.

Appendix A

DPMax for LCS Analysis of Human and Cow Insulin

The A chains of human and cow (bovine) insulin were compared to obtain their longest common subsequences so as to produce the LCS between them for further investigation. Such investigations could be similarities in structure and function between the two peptides and also phylogenesis.

HUMAN INSULIN
======================

```
>4EWX:A|PDBID|CHAIN|SEQUENCE
GIVEQCCTSICSLYQLENYCN
>4EWX:B|PDBID|CHAIN|SEQUENCE
FVNQHLCGSHLVEALYLVCGERGFFYTPKT
>4EWX:C|PDBID|CHAIN|SEQUENCE
GIVEQCCTSICSLYQLENYCN
>4EWX:D|PDBID|CHAIN|SEQUENCE
FVNQHLCGSHLVEALYLVCGERGFFYTPKT
```

COW (BOVINE) INSULIN
=====================

```
>4E7T:A|PDBID|CHAIN|SEQUENCE
GIVEQCCASVCSLYQLENYCN
>4E7T:B|PDBID|CHAIN|SEQUENCE
FVNQHLCGSHLVEALYLVCGERGFFYTPKA
>4E7T:C|PDBID|CHAIN|SEQUENCE
GIVEQCCASVCSLYQLENYCN
>4E7T:D|PDBID|CHAIN|SEQUENCE
FVNQHLCGSHLVEALYLVCGERGFFYTPKA
```

=======================

The Text output follows.

Longest Common Subsequence using Dynamic Programming
Copyright (c) 2009 Desmond Ogirri. All Rights Reserved.

1. Input

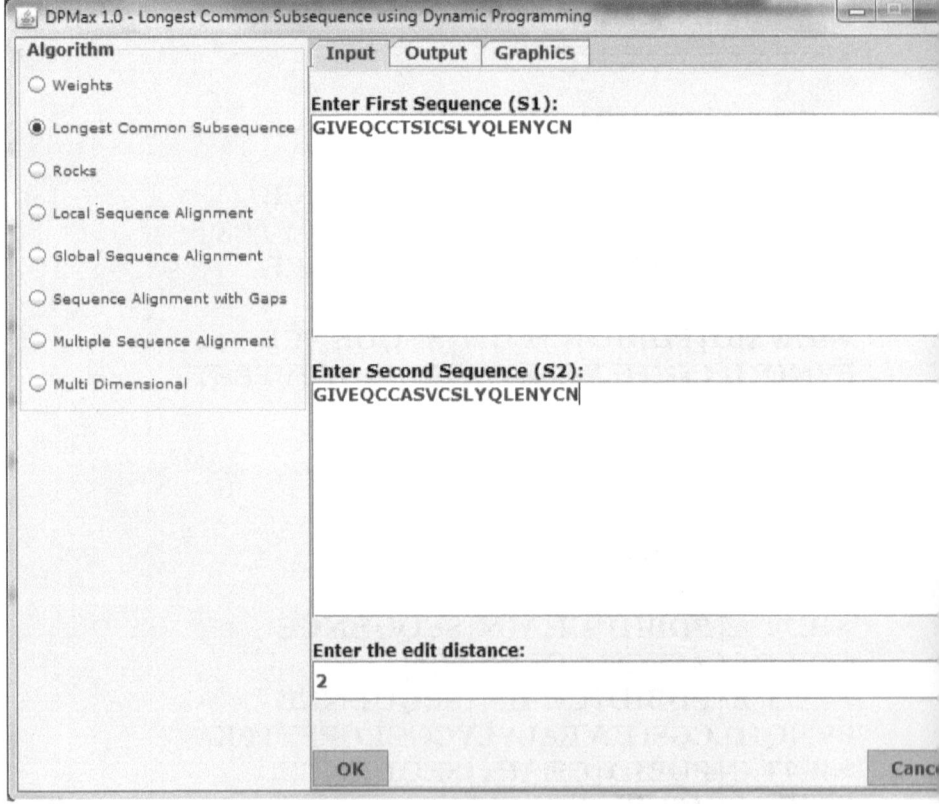

Sequence 1 = GIVEQCCTSICSLYQLENYCN [21-mer]
Sequence 2 = GIVEQCCASVCSLYQLENYCN [21-mer]
The alignment is:

GIVEQCC-TS-ICSLYQLENYCN
GIVEQCCA-SV-CSLYQLENYCN
The alignment edit distance is 4
The LCS through the matrix as obtained by Dynamic Programming is...
GIVEQCCSCSLYQLENYCN
The score of the LCS is 19
The length of the LCS is 19

2. Output

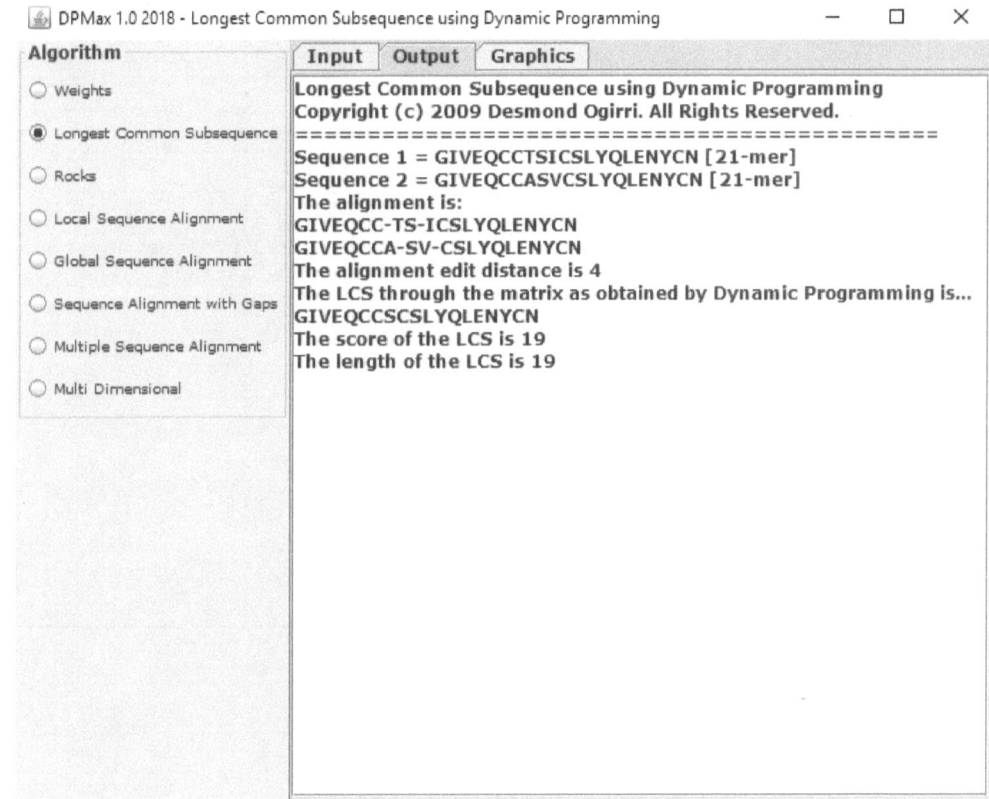

3. The Graphical output is shown below.

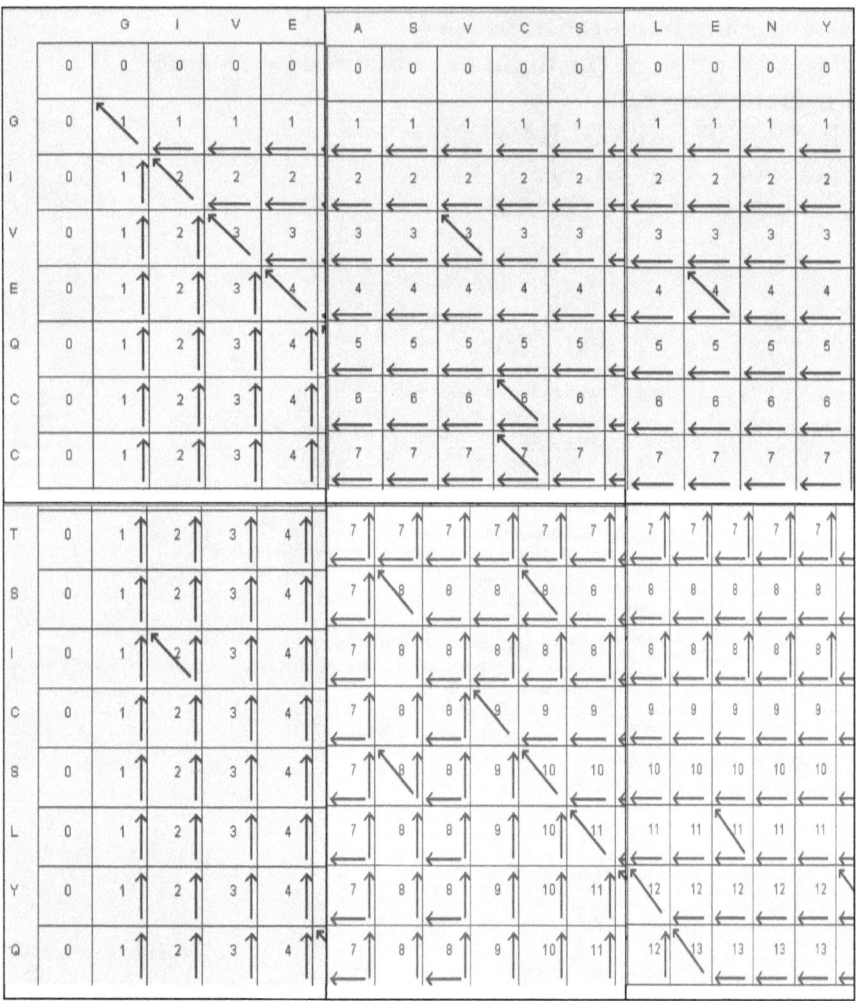

L	0	↑1	↑2	↑3	↑4	↑7 ←	↑8	↑8 ←	↑9	↑10	↖14	14 ←	14 ←	14 ←
E	0	↑1	↑2	↑3	↖4	↑7 ←	↑8	↑8 ←	↑9	↑10	↑14	↖15	15 ←	15 ←
N	0	↑1	↑2	↑3	↑4	↑7 ←	↑8	↑8 ←	↑9	↑10	↑14	↑15	↖16	16 ←
Y	0	↑1	↑2	↑3	↑4	↑7 ←	↑8	↑8 ←	↑9	↑10	↑14	↑15	↑16	↖17
C	0	↑1	↑2	↑3	↑4	↑7 ←	↑8	↖8	↘9	↑10	↑14	↑15	↑16	↑17
N	0	↑1	↑2	↑3	↑4	↑7 ←	↑8	↑8 ←	↑9	↑10	↑14	↑15	↖16	↑17

Appendix B

DPMax for LCS Analysis of Two Short DNA Sequences

The text and graphical results are shown below.

1. Input tab

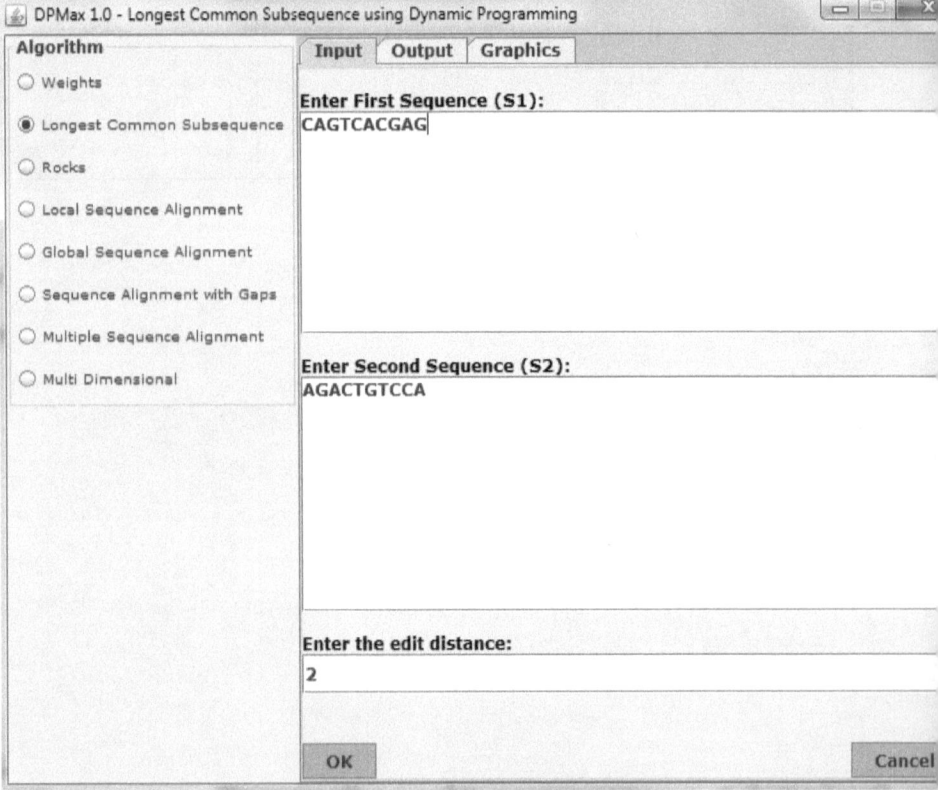

2. Output

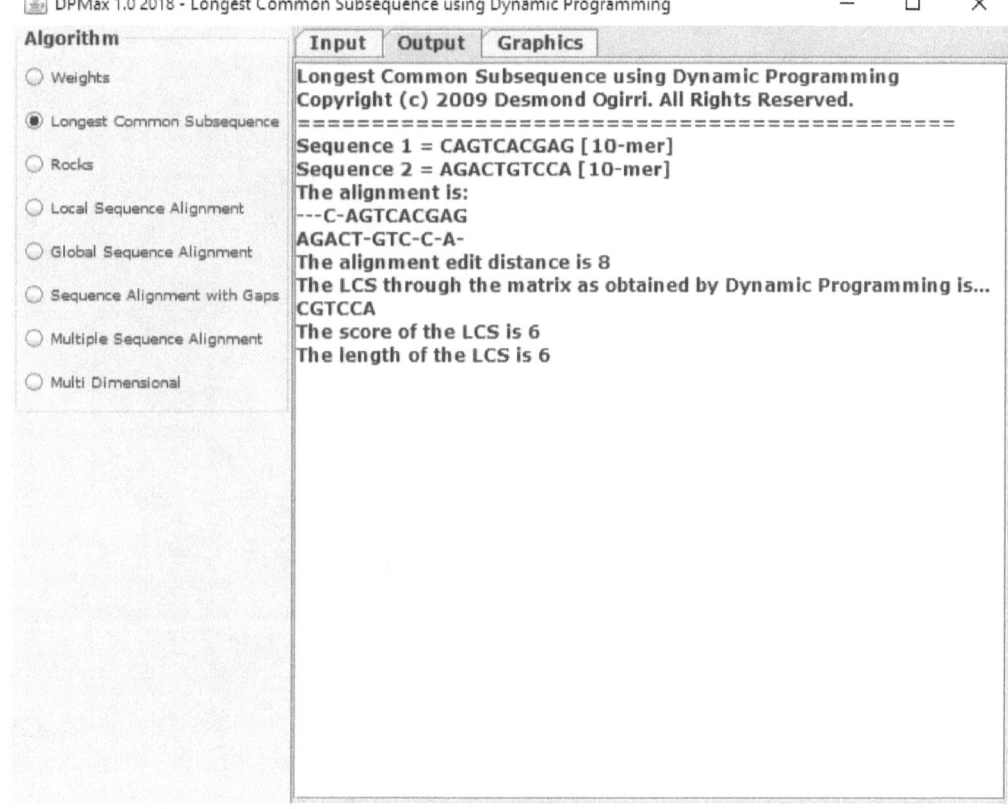

3. Graphics tab

BLANK PAGE

Part 2

The Longest and Shortest Paths Problems using Weights

CONTENTS

PART 1
CONTENTS .... Error! Bookmark not defined.
ABSTRACT 5
INTRODUCTION 8
METHODS AND EXPERIMENTS 22
RESULTS 24
DISCUSSION 58
ACKNOWLEDGEMENT 67
CITATIONS 68
Appendix A 71
Appendix B 76

PART 2
CONTENTS 81
ABSTRACT 83
INTRODUCTION 84
METHODS AND EXPERIMENTS 89
RESULTS 91
DISCUSSION 115
ACKNOWLEDGEMENT 120
CITATIONS 121
Appendix A 124

ABSTRACT

The first part of this paper detailed the workings of the LCS module of DPMax version 1.0. DPMax is a software tool that was written to implement and display the ways common dynamic programming (DP) algorithms work. These DP algorithms not only returned the text output of the execution of their algorithms, but also displayed in a graphical format the resulting matrixes after the execution of those algorithms. DPMax contains two fully finished modules – Weights and Longest Common Subsequence.

The version 1.0 of DPMax for Weights implements the DP algorithm that solves the problem of the longest paths between 2 points given a series of values. These values represent the distances between adjacent cities or geographical locations. It is modelled closely on the Longest and Shortest Paths Problem as in the *Traveling Salesman* and *Manhattan Tourist Problems* which are detailed in many Mathematical and Computer Science texts (Reingold et. al., Dasgupta et. al.).

DPMax for Weights makes the function of achieving the longest and shortest paths easy to comprehend and understand, just like its LCS counterpart, with its text and graphic outputs. The text output with weights simply displays the pairs of rows and columns which represent the edges and vertices of the graph used to solve the problem and then display the graphical solution.

INTRODUCTION

So much has been said about DP in the first part of the paper in the writeup on the LCS module. So, this part of the paper will go straight to the point.

Dynamic programming is a mathematical-cum-computer scientific method to solve certain kinds of optimization problems. These unique problems must have certain properties (Bellman) including:

1. It should obey the principle of optimality which means that
   a. It should comprise overlapping subproblems
   b. It should exhibit an overlapping substructure

2. It should be visualizable as a matrix comprising smaller problems with each one having the same or very similar properties, like the decision variables to be solved, as the main problem. In other words, each of the constituent problems should be a mini-version, or mini-repetition, of the big one.

As soon as the dynamic programming is confirmed, an appropriate DP algorithm must be sought to solve the problem.

The two methods used for the implementation of DP are the classic method (aka top-down or memoization method) and the bottom-up method (sometimes called the tabulation method). DPMax employs the bottom-up method for its modules.

It should be noted that there will be no repetitions from the LCS paper. So, comments shall be made in this paper only when there is a marked difference in a particular section of the two modules.

Solving the Longest Paths Problem using Graph Weights (The Manhattan Tourist Problem)

The problem of the Manhattan Tourist lies in making a decision – how to traverse the many possible paths between the 2 extreme and opposing points while seeing as many tourist attractions as possible. From the northwesternmost point (called the *source* vertex) the traveller must eventually get to the southeasternmost point (called the *sink* vertex). The distance from one vertex to another is called a weight. The weight of a path from the source vertex to the sink vertex is calculated as the sum of weights of its edges. These weights are the total number of attractions which the tourist desires to see.

The intersections between the streets that run from west-east and north-south form the vertices while the edges are the streets running north-south and west-east which intersect with one another. This structure of edges and vertices is a grid-like graph, *G*. The horizontal edges in G run from west to east and the vertical one run from north to south. All the edges have weights which are the length of the streets as they run from one vertex, or intersection, to another. A continuous sequence of edges is called a path. The length of each path is the sum of all the weights of the edges in that path.

What is the definition of the Manhattan Tourist Problem?

To find the greatest (maximum) number of attractions between the source and sink vertices. This path is the longest path, and the largest weight, between the 2 vertices (i.e. the start and finish points) (Dasgupta et. al.).

Input: A graph with weighted edges from west to east and north to south.

Output: The longest path with largest weight, L, through the grid, G, from the source to sink vertices.

Solution

1. The total number of paths running from west to east represent the number of rows in the grid while the number of paths running from north to south are the columns in the grid in the graph.

Let the number of rows = n, while

the number of columns = m,

We are to find $L_{n, m}$, the length of the longest path with the maximum weight through G

2. The source vertex is at position $G[0, 0]$ of the grid while the sink vertex is at $G[n-1, m-1]$.

3. The total number of subproblems is ($n \times m$) which represents the total number of all vertices in G. We must start by finding all the weights of vertices along the first row, $G[0, j]$, and first column, $G[i, 0]$. Because the tourists can only move eastwards from the source to sink, then $G[0, j]$ (for $0 <= j <= m$) is the sum of weights of the first j city blocks. Likewise, $G[i, 0]$ (for $0 <= i <= n$) is the sum of weights of the first i city blocks, because the tourists can only move southwards from source towards sink.

4. Now that we have found the base case of the Weights algorithm, we must now proceed to find the lengths of the paths between the vertices along the rows and columns. This can be solved by a recurrence that takes into consideration the edges and vertices and the movements between them. We know that getting to any vertex in the grid can only occur by moving southwards, (to $G[i, j]$ from $G[i-1, j]$), or eastwards (to $G[i, j]$ from $G[i, j-1]$), through the grid. We can formulate the solution through the subproblems of the grid as:

$L_{i, j}$ = max ($L_{i,-1, j}$ + weight of the edge between $G[i -1, j]$ and $G[i, j]$,

$L_{i, j-1}$ + weight of the edge between $G[i , j-1]$ and $G[i, j]$,)

5. With the foregoing, we can formulate the Longest Path by Weights (Manhattan Tourist) algorithm

function LongestPathByWeights ()

$H[]$ – A 2-Dimensional array of weights of edges that run from west to east (horizontal)

$V[]$ – A 2-Dimensional array of weights of edges that run from north to south (vertical)

n = length of the array $H[]$

m = length of the array $V[]$

(1) $G[0, 0] = 0$

(2)   for i = 0 to n

            $G[i, 0] = G[i -1, 0] + V[i, 0]$

(3)   for j = 0 to n

            $G[0, j] = G[j -1, 0] + H[0, j]$

(4)   for i = 1 to n

(5)   for j = 1 to m

(6) $L_{i, j} = \max (L_{i-1, j} + V[i, j], L_{i, j-1} + H[i, j])$

(7)   return $L_{n, m}$

6. Again, as in the LCS module, careful attention must be taken so as not to do a simple max() function to obtain the larger path between two possible paths. If two paths have equal lengths, both paths must be marked as possible paths to the optimal solutions. This may mean that we have multiple optimal paths to the sink vertex, that is, the ending point for the tourist.

7. Now that we have the optimal path or paths, we have to develop a backtracking algorithm to obtain those paths from source to sink.

Computational Complexity

We have already established that we have a fixed number of subproblems obtained as the product of the rows and columns, that is, $n \times m$. the beginning of the Weights function takes as input 2 2-Dimensional arrays, H and V. Both are arrays of arrays of the weights of the Horizontal (west-east) and Vertical (north-south) edges, respectively. From lines (1) to (3) are the initialization conditions of the algorithm. Lines (4) and (5) are the outer and inner loops over the horizontal and vertical arrays, respectively. The runtime of the first loop, over the horizontal array of west-east weights, is $O(n)$, while the runtime of the second loop over the vertical array of north-south weights is $O(m)$.

The basic operation within the inner loop is a max() function which costs a simple constant $O(1)$ time. Even if there is a check for equal paths, the operation cost doesn't change, it is still constant. So, the total runtime through the ManhattanTourist function is $O(nm) \times O(1)$, which comes to $O(nm)$. If both rows and columns have the same length such that $n = m$, then the runtime is $O(n^2)$.

The backtracking function should be as simple as possible because the complete backtracking operation costs as much as exponential. But this implementation is a modified backtracking operation that obtains only 1 optimal solution path to avoid the usual complexities with this operation. It starts from the sink vertex and follows the path of its subproblems of solutions until it gets to the source vertex and then it exits, returning the optimal longest path from source to sink vertices. As in the LCS, each vertex at $G[i, j]$, has a store of which prior vertex provided its solution. There are no diagonal vertices here unlike in the LCS, so there can only be a path from the north vertex, $G[i-1, j]$, or the west vertex, $G[i, j-1]$. The modified algorithm runs in $O(k)$ where k is the number of vertices (intersections) traversed to obtain the longest path $L_{n, m}$.

METHODS AND EXPERIMENTS

DPMax for Weights was used to compute the modified Manhattan Tourist Problem by finding the longest paths between 2 points – a starting point and a finish point.

The grid was a 4-by-4 grid with 4 rows and 4 columns. The number of rows and columns were input in the Input tab and the 'OK' button was pressed. The GUI produced a dialog input box that prompted for each of the west-east edge weights one by one, specifying the particular intersection of rows (row i and row i+1) that should be entered. At soon as the input box captured all the west-east weights data, it prompted for the same weights for the north-south edges one by one.

Once that was completed, the software performed the computation of the Weights algorithm as detailed earlier. The Output tab would then have the results of the analysis in text format.

Also, the Graphical tab contained the graph matrix that was produced by the 4x4 grid specified in the input tab. The grid comprises circles connected by arrows or lines and then numbers along the arrows or lines or in the circles.

The solution to the grid is displayed in 3 parts –

1. The lines or arrows that connect the circles are the weights of edges that represent the streets of the city,

2. The circles represent the vertices between the edges. They are the intersections between the streets. The first circle at the northwesternmost end of the graph is the source vertex, and it is the starting point for the tourist, and,

3. The numbers by the edges represent the weights of the edges. The numbers in the circles are the solutions to the vertex subproblems. They are the sum of the longest path leading to that particular vertex.

3. The lines connection the vertices may be either one of 2 forms

a.) An arrow pointing from one vertex to another indicating that the vertex the arrow is pointing to is a solution to the vertex it is pointing to.

b.) A line connecting 2 vertices indicating that it's not a solution to the connecting vertex.

There could be multiple arrows pointing to a vertex meaning that both connecting vertices have produced solutions to that vertex. In a simple grid, a visual backtracking operation could be performed to find the longest paths from the source to the sink.

The arrows and numbers shown in each cell were produced via repeated calls to the Java Graphics methods draw() and others to render the images on a JPanel canvas as follows:

1. The grid is drawn as a 2-dimensional array of arrays of edges running from west-east and north-south, and vertices intersecting the edges.
2. The vertices of the graph are drawn as circles with each connected to surrounding vertices in the matrix by edges.
3. The edges were drawn as line connecting the vertices. the west-east weights are drawn first, then the north-south weights are drawn.
4. The solutions of the vertices were computed and arrows were drawn to signify what vertices are the solutions to others, if any exist.
5. The numbers are drawn beside or above the edges to show the weights of edges and also inside the circular vertices to indicate the solution for each vertex.

When completed, a grid of possibilities appears for the tourist to traverse the longest path of maximum interactions, which is the optimal solution to the problem (Dasgupta *et al.*, Chap.6).

RESULTS

DPMax for Weights creates an $n \times m$ matrix, a grid of intersecting edges and vertices, comprising a graph $GR[n, m]$. The input into the GUI was a set of 2-Dimensional array of weights – the first was the array of arrays of west-east weights while the second one was an array of arrays of north-south weights. The final set of weights which were input by the user were displayed on the respective text areas in the Input tab of the Weights module.

The length of the west-east 2-D array is n, while the length of the north-south array is m. All the input values must be integers because that is the expected input. The first vertex, the source, has the value of 0. This is because it is the starting point and has no incoming edges. The sink vertex contains the longest path as computed by the algorithm.

There were two sets of experimental grids created with DPMax – one was a 4x4 grid while the other one was a 5x5 matrix. For the sake of brevity, the results of the 4x4 matrix is presented here. The results of the other, larger, grid is in the Appendices. It should be noted that the software can create much larger grids.

The Results for 4x4 Weights Grid

The result of a 4x4 matrix of edge weights and vertices was determined. The output of the results was displayed in text format on the 'Output' tab and the graphical display was presented on the 'Graphics' tab.

The Input tab is shown in the figure below, and it shows the number of rows and columns specified in the appropriate input box in the Weights GUI.

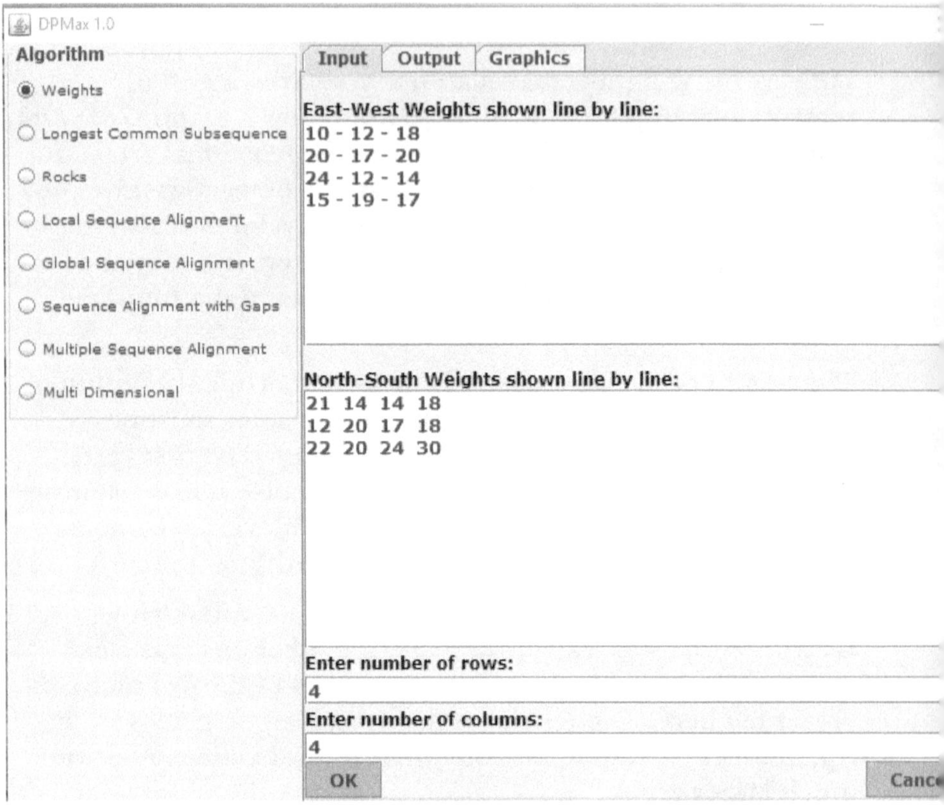

Figure 1: The Input tab of the Weights module. It shows the input number of rows and columns. The values of the west-east and north-south weights input by the user are displayed in the upper and lower text areas, respectively.

The next figure shows the Java Input dialog box which accepts the input values for the weights of both west-east and north-south edges.

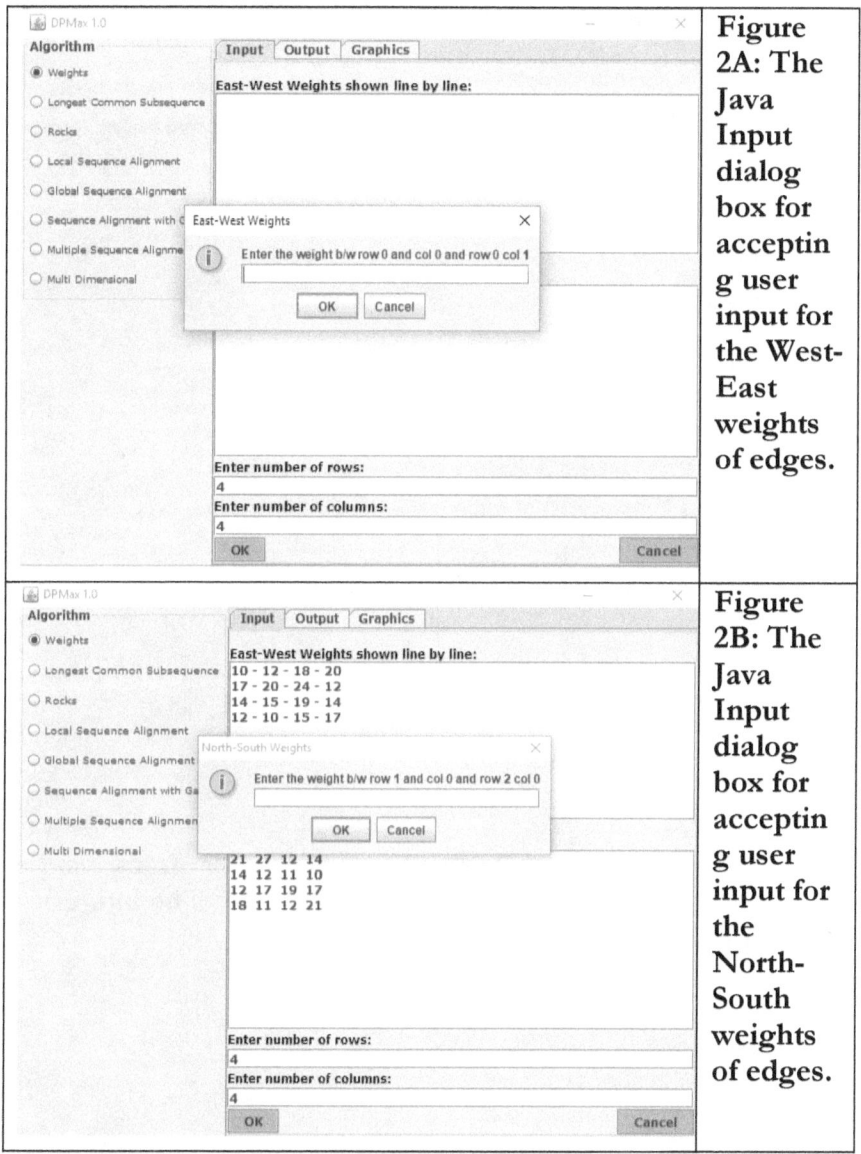

Figure 2A: The Java Input dialog box for accepting user input for the West-East weights of edges.

Figure 2B: The Java Input dialog box for accepting user input for the North-South weights of edges.

Once the user input is complete, the Output tab will contain the results of the algorithm. This result would be the longest path between the source and sink vertices in text in the format, [0, 0]…[i, j]…[n, m]. The longest path from the start

93

to end of the 4x4 grid matrix is shown in the next figure that shows the results of the Output tab of the Weights module.

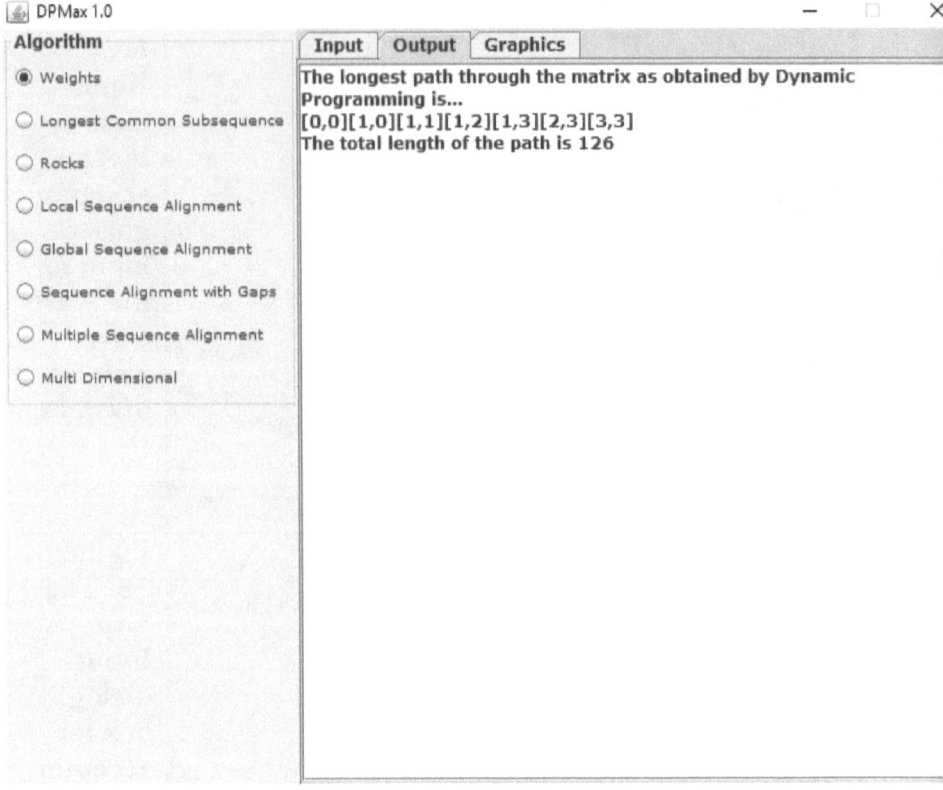

Figure 3: The Output tab of the Weights module. It shows the longest path through the matrix of the 4x4 grid. The longest path through the grid, $L_{n,\,m}$, is 126.

Graphics Output

The figure below is the graphical display of the 4x4 grid produced by DPMax.

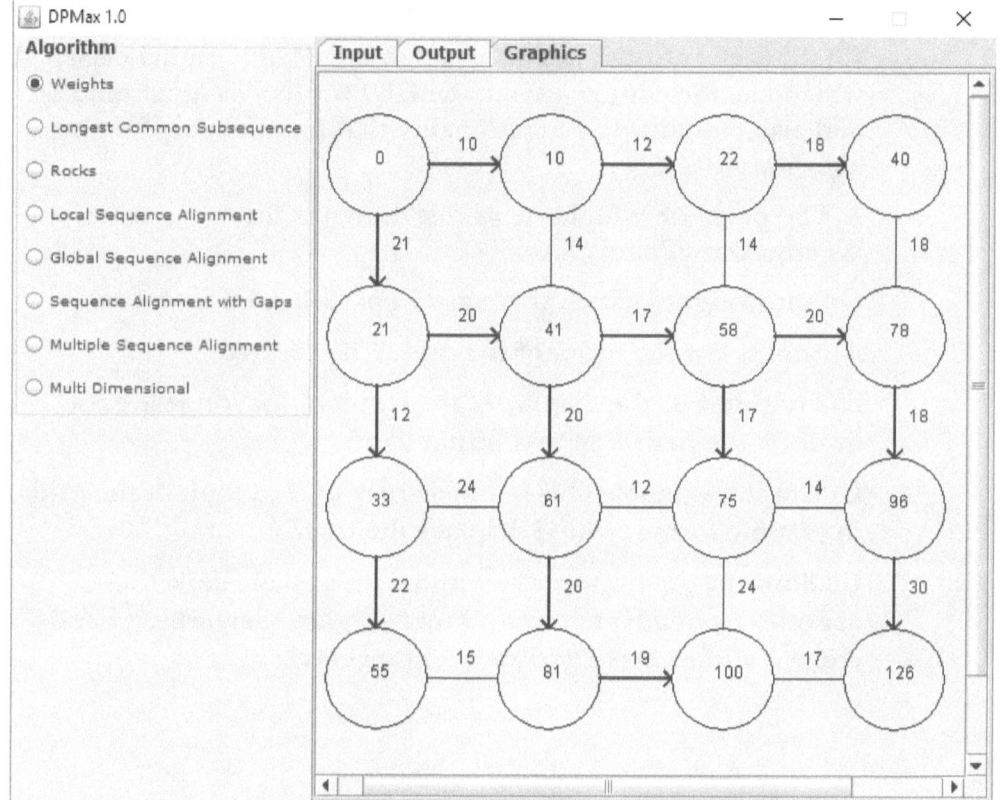

Figure 4: The Graphics tab of the Weights module. The matrix displays a 4-rows-x-4-columns grid with the optimal solution at the position G[n-1, m-1]. The longest path ([0,0] [1,0] [1,1] [1,2] [1,3] [2,3] [3,3]) has the value of 126.

The longest path is ([0,0] [1,0] [1,1] [1,2] [1,3] [2,3] [3,3]) has a value of 126. The source vertex the first one and has a value of 0. The last vertex, the sink, has a value of 126. The vertex array of the longest path is ([0] [21] [41] [58] [78] [96] [126]).

Architecture, High-level Design and Program Flow

The architecture, design and program flow for the Weights module are the same as the LCS module. The Object classes, however, are different and they are as follows:

1. DPMaxController makes a call to DynProgWeights class, which has the code to create the GUI for the Weights module and also contains the functionality that handles the Weights algorithm itself.

2. The panel on which the grid is drawn is the WeightsDrawPanel class.

On the Weights panel, there are 3 possible GUI interactions

A) Input: For the input of the grid to be created.

B) Output: For the display of the result of the longest path through the matrix in text format, and,

C) Graphics panel: This is the display of the result of the grid in graphic format which displays the matrix.

Clicking on the button 'OK' on the input page calls the actionPerformed() method of the Weights View which hands control to the class DynProgWeights class.

The *DPMax for Weights* Module

The Weights Module Methods and Functions

The main class that contains the Weights module view and functionality is the DynProgWeights class. The *dpg* object is an instance of, and encapsulates the functionality within, the DPGraphics class.

The Input tab has an 'OK' button which when pressed triggers an action event that is sent to the actionPerformed() method in this class. Once in this method, the class reads the 2 numbers for rows and columns. The class then builds a grid according to the specified number of rows and columns. It uses these numbers to create an input dialog box which prompts the user to enter the west-east weights according to the rows and columns needed to build the grid.

Once it does that, it calls the method doDPWeights() which reads the number of rows and columns and creates the grid matrix based on those numbers. The grid is just a list of objects of type Cell as encapsulated within that class. This means that each vertex in the matrix is of type Cell and these cells are connected by lines or arrows.

Initializing the matrix scores

The doDPWeights() method then calls the method initialize() to initialize the matrix and it does so by creating each vertex cell (the first of which is created with an initial score of 0) and positioning them in the matrix. The initialize() method promptly calls helper method initializeScores() which will set the scores for each cell in that grid for the first row, west-east weights, and first column, the north-south weights. The initialize() method will first present the user with the option input box that will accept the values of the edge weights from the user. Once that is done, it parses them as integers and places them in the appropriate 2-Dimensional arrays – one for the west-east and another for the north-south. At this point, initialize() calls initializeScores() which will compute the scores for the vertices in first row, $G[0, j]$, and the first column, $G[i, 0]$. Then all the other vertices in the grid's matrix must be filled.

Filling the LCS Matrix: fillMatrix()

Once the initial scores have been fixed in each cell in the matrix, doDPWeights() then calls another method fillMatrix() to actually fill the matrix with the solution of each cell until it reaches the optimal solution at the sink vertex. And because this is the bottom-up approach, just like the LCS module, it starts by solving the cells which are the smaller problems and then uses the solutions for those cells that have been solved to find the solution for the overlapping cells which are larger problems. But unlike the LCS algorithm, it progresses downwards towards the south and eastwards until it solves the sink cell which is the final vertex/intersection.

This method, implements the routines of the Weights recurrence algorithm. It begins by going into a set of *for* loops thereby incurring the bulk of the runtime cost. The first loop iterates over the array of west-east weights. The second, inner loop, iterates over the array of north-south weights. Within this code, the $O(nm)$ runtime of the algorithm occurs. The basic operation of solving each subproblem is done by the helper method that is called within this fillMatrix() method. That method, fillCell(), performs basic operations in constant $O(1)$ time.

By the end of fillMatrix(), each vertex of the matrix has been given a solution score and the final vertex has been scored. fillMatrix() delegates that functionality to another method fillCell() to do the actual cell filling. fillCell() is a helper method which fills cells of the matrix by the Weights algorithm being used. After being solved, every cell is then connected to the surrounding cells – above, below, left, or right. Every cell must know its relative cells in the optimal substructure of *G*.

Filling each cell: The fillCell() method

The function of the fillCell() method is quite straightforward. It is an overloaded method which takes as parameter 3 Weights cells. These cells are the current cell, the cell above and the cell to the left of the current.

With these parameters, it builds connections and pointers between the cells as needed. It connects each cell to its surrounding cell and creates pointers that indicate which cell or cells provided the solution to the current cell. Every cell has pointers set to indicate where its solution came from and every cell also contains a class member which is an instance of java.util.Map where it stores all its connections to its surrounding cells.

Once the matrix has been filled, we know its optimal solution in the sink vertex. But the task is far from completed. We still need to find the actual path that ends in the optimal solution at the sink. This is the final step in many dynamic programming programs and for the Longest Path by Weights Problem, it is what gives us the actual path that we have been searching for – the longest path it will take for the Manhattan Tourist to experience as many attractions as possible. All this is done through something called a *traceback* – a backtracking technique for finding the final solution of our Weights matrix that contains the optimal solution so found. It is aptly called a traceback because it does exactly what its name implies – it walks backwards through the matrix starting at the optimal solution at the sink, to the beginning of the matrix at the source.

The Backtrack function: doTraceback()

This code for the doTraceback() function is quite the same as the LCS. The only differences are: firstly, here the function returns the longest path from source to sink as a String object which contains a series of vertices expressed as intersections of rows and columns ([row, column]). Also, the final vertex, the source, is inserted at the front of the String once the traceback reaches the beginning of the grid. Once the traceback is complete, then the longest path from source to sink would have been achieved.

This traceback is a simplified version of a typical traceback. It starts at the sink vertex and regresses through the list of previous cells until it gets to the end of the list where if finds a null cell or a cell with a score less than or equal to 0. Once there is a null or zero/subzero score, it has reached the end of this list, or at the source vertex and it exits the while loop. One it does that, it inserts the source vertex at the start of the list. The traceback queries every cell to get the previous cell, that is, the cell which provided the solution to the current cell. Once it gets that information of that current cell, it sets the previous cell as the current cell and the process repeats itself. It keeps on looping until if finds a current cell which has the previous cell as null or cell score not greater than 0. By this time, it has reached the source vertex. The previous cell could be the cell to the left (west) or the cell above (north).

```java
public static void initialize() {
    //get the weights that we need for the whole table
    String sWeight = "";
    Cell prevCell = null;
    Cell currCell = null;
    Map<String, Cell> prevCellMap = new HashMap<String, Cell>();
    for (int row = 0; row < matrix.length; row++) {
        for (int col = 0; col < matrix[row].length; col++)
        {
            matrix[row][col] = new Cell(row, col);
            if(row == 0 && col > 0){
                currCell = matrix[row][col];
                prevCell = matrix[row][col-1];
                currCell.setPrevCell(prevCell);
                prevCellMap.put(Constant.CELL_TO_LEFT, prevCell);
                currCell.setPrevCellMap(prevCellMap);
            }

            if(col == 0 && row > 0){
                currCell = matrix[row][col];
                prevCell = matrix[row-1][col];
                currCell.setPrevCell(prevCell);
                prevCellMap.put(Constant.CELL_ABOVE, prevCell);
                currCell.setPrevCellMap(prevCellMap);
            }

        }
    }

    rows = "";
    //fill up the west-east weights
    for (int row = 0; row < row_weights.length; row++) {
        for (int col = 0; col < row_weights[row].length; col++) {
            try {
                sWeight = JOptionPane.showInputDialog(null,
```

```java
                            "Enter the weight
b/w row " + row
                            + " and col " + col
+ " and row "
                            + row + " col " +
                            (col+1), "West-
                            East Weights",

            JOptionPane.INFORMATION_MESSAGE);
                    } catch (HeadlessException e) {
                            // TODO Auto-generated catch block
                            e.printStackTrace();
                            return;
                    }


                    try {
                            row_weights[row][col] =
                            Integer.parseInt(sWeight);
                    } catch (NumberFormatException e) {
                            e.printStackTrace();
                            return;
                    }

                    if(col < nCols - 2)
                            rows += sWeight + " - ";
                    else
                            rows += sWeight;
            }
        rows += "\n";
    }

            cols = "";
            String temp = "";
            //then the north-south weights
            for (int row = 1; row < col_weights.length; row++) {
                    for (int col = 0; col < col_weights[row-1].length; col++) {
```

```java
            try {
                sWeight = JOptionPane.showInputDialog(null,
                        "Enter the weight b/w row " + (row-1)
                        + " and col " + col + "
                        and row " + row +
                        " col " + col, "North-South Weights",
                        JOptionPane.INFORMATION_MESSAGE);
            } catch (HeadlessException e) {
                // TODO Auto-generated catch block
                e.printStackTrace();
                return;
            }

            try {
                col_weights[row-1][col] = Integer.parseInt(sWeight);
            } catch (NumberFormatException e) {
                e.printStackTrace();
                return;
            }

            cols += sWeight + " ";
        }
        cols += "\n";
    }

    txtArea1.setText(rows);
    txtArea2.setText(cols);
    dpg.setMatrix(matrix);
    dpg.setRow_weights(row_weights);
    dpg.setCol_weights(col_weights);

    initializeScores();
```

}

```
public static void initializeScores(){
    //start by setting the first cell score to 0
    matrix[0][0].setScore(0);
    int score = 0;

    //set the scores for each cell
    //at first column ie column 0 and row row
    for(int row = 1; row < nRows; row++){
        score = matrix[row-1][0].getScore() +
        col_weights[row-1][0];
        matrix[row][0].setScore(score);
    }

    //then set the scores for each cell
    //at first row ie column col and row 0
    for(int col = 1; col < nCols; col++){
        score = matrix[0][col-1].getScore() +
        row_weights[0][col-1];
        matrix[0][col].setScore(score);
    }

}

public static void fillMatrix() {
    int aboveWt, leftWt = 0;
    for (int row = 1; row < matrix.length; row++) {
        for (int col = 1; col < matrix[row].length; col++) {
            Cell currentCell = matrix[row][col];
            Cell cellAbove = matrix[row - 1][col];
            Cell cellToLeft = matrix[row][col - 1];

            aboveWt = col_weights[row-1][col];
            leftWt = row_weights[row][col-1];

            fillCell(currentCell, cellAbove, cellToLeft,
```

```java
                    aboveWt, leftWt);
            }
        }
    }


        public static void fillCell(Cell currentCell, Cell cellAbove,
                    Cell cellToLeft, int aboveWt, int leftWt) {
                int aboveScore = cellAbove.getScore() + aboveWt;
                int leftScore = cellToLeft.getScore() + leftWt;
                Map<String, Cell> prevCellMap =
                                new
                            HashMap<String, Cell>();
                int cellScore = 0;
                Cell prevCell;
                if (leftScore >= aboveScore) {
                  if (leftScore > aboveScore) {
                    cellScore = leftScore;
                    prevCell = cellToLeft;

                prevCellMap.put(Constant.CELL_TO_LEFT,
                cellToLeft);
                    } else {
                        //ideally if they are the same the two
                        //should both be set as pointers
                    //leftScore == aboveScore
                    cellScore = leftScore;
                    prevCell = cellToLeft;

        prevCellMap.put(Constant.CELL_TO_LEFT,
        cellToLeft);

prevCellMap.put(Constant.CELL_ABOVE, cellAbove);
                    }
                } else {//aboveScore > leftScore

                    cellScore = aboveScore;
                    prevCell = cellAbove;
```

```
                prevCellMap.put(Constant.CELL_ABOVE, cellAbove);
            }
                currentCell.setScore(cellScore);
                currentCell.setPrevCell(prevCell);
                currentCell.setPrevCellMap(prevCellMap);
    }
        public static String doTraceback() {
                StringBuffer buf = new StringBuffer();
                Cell currentCell = matrix[nRows - 1][nCols - 1];
                Cell prevCell;
                int row = 0;
                int col = 0;
                score = currentCell.getScore();
                while(currentCell != null &&
                        currentCell.getScore() > 0)
                {
                        prevCell = currentCell.getPrevCell();
                        row = currentCell.getRow();
                        col = currentCell.getCol();
                        buf.insert(0, "[" + row + "," + col + "]");

                        currentCell = prevCell;

                }

                buf.insert(0, "[0,0]");
                return buf.toString();
        }

        public void doDPWeights(){
                matrix = new Cell[nRows][nCols];
                row_weights = new int[nRows][nCols-1];
                col_weights = new int[nRows][nCols];

                //now compute the other weights
                initialize();
                fillMatrix();
                String wtsStr = doTraceback();
```

```
            String results = "The longest path through the
matrix as " +
            "obtained by Dynamic Programming is...\n" +
wtsStr
                             + "\n" +
                         "The total length of the
path is " + score;
            String ruler =
"\n================================
========\n";
            txtArea3.append(ruler + results);
    }
```

The Graphical output

The graphical output was also created within the same doDPWeights() function that created the functionality of the non-graphical output. The graphical functionality is encapsulated within the DPGraphics class which serves as both a panel and event listener that handles the high-level event listening and actions and contains the main drawing panel. The DPGraphics class has an overloaded constructor to handle either the LCS module or the Weights module.

It receives the user interaction from the container app deals with those action or mouse events. This DPGraphics object that handles Weights functionality delegates the heavy lifting drawing to another panel, the main drawing panel called WeightsDrawPanel. It is this class that contains all the drawing capabilities that draw the Weights matrix. It does most of its drawing in a method called drawMatrix() which takes as input parameters, array of arrays of Weights Cell objects.

Drawing the Weights Matrix

Drawing the grid of the Weights matrix occurs very similar to the way LCS is drawn. The vertices are drawn first by drawing the cells of the matrix. Then the west-east edges are drawn followed by the north-south weights. Then the weights are drawn as numbers beside and above the edges and numbers in the vertices as solutions are computed. The arrows are drawn as the solutions are produced and longest paths to the sink are found.

```
public void drawMatrix(Cell[][] matrix, int row_weights[][],
            int col_weights[][]){

        if (matrix == null ||
            row_weights == null || col_weights ==
        null)
            return;
        int x = 30;
```

```java
                        int y = 30;
                        int x1 = 0;
                        int x2 = 0;
                        int y1 = 0;
                        int y2 = 0;
                        int x3 = 0;
                        int y3 = 0;
                        int width = 50;
                        int height = 50;
                        int space = 100;
                        int row;
                        int col;
                        String score;
                        Stroke prevStk;
                        Stroke boldStk = new BasicStroke(2f);
                        String wts = "";
                        Map<String, Cell> prevCellMap = null;
                        area = new Dimension();
                        g2d = (Graphics2D)gr;
                        Cell[][] copyMatrix = matrix;
                        row = copyMatrix.length;
                        col = copyMatrix[0].length;
                        int lastScore = copyMatrix[row-1][col-
1].getScore();
                        String sScr = String.valueOf(lastScore);
                            int dim = (sScr.length() * 2) +
                            g2d.getFontMetrics().getHeight());
                        width += dim;
                        height += dim;
                        space += dim;
                        for (row = 0; row < copyMatrix.length; row++)
{
                            for (col = 0; col < copyMatrix[row].length;
col++) {
                                Cell currentCell = copyMatrix[row][col];
                                Cell prevCell = currentCell.getPrevCell();
                                prevCellMap =
currentCell.getPrevCellMap();

                                if(row == 0 && col > 0)
```

```
                    prevCellMap = null;
                if(col == 0 && row > 0)
                    prevCellMap = null;
                prevStk = g2d.getStroke();
                    //if the prev cell is null just draw the
            current cell
                if (prevCellMap == null ||
prevCellMap.isEmpty())
                {
                    g2d.drawOval(x, y, width, height);

                    if(col < matrix[row].length - 1 && row
== 0){
                        x1 = x + width;
                        y1 = y + (height/2);
                        x2 = x + space ;
                        y2 = y1;
                        g2d.setStroke(boldStk);
                        g2d.drawLine(x1, y1, x2, y2);
                            //draw the west-east weights
                            wts = String.valueOf(
row_weights[row][col] );
                            x3 = (( x1 + x2 ) / 2 ) -
(wts.length()*2);
                            y3 = y1 - 10;

                        g2d.drawString(wts, x3, y3);
                        //now draw the arrows
                            x1 = x2 - 5;
                            y1 = y2 - 5;
                            x3 = x2 - 5;
                            y3 = y2 + 5;
                            g2d.drawLine(x1, y1, x2, y2);
                            g2d.drawLine(x2, y2, x3, y3);

                        g2d.setStroke(prevStk);
                    }

                    //if the row is not 0 draw the north-
south line
```

```java
if (row > 0 && col == 0){
    //draw the north-south line
    x1 = x + (width/2);
    y1 = y - space + height;
    x2 = x1;
    y2 = y1 + space - height;
    g2d.setStroke(boldStk);
    g2d.drawLine(x1, y1, x2, y2);

    //draw the north-south weights
    //g2d.setStroke(prevStk);
    wts = String.valueOf( col_weights[row-1][col] );
    x3 = x1 + 10;
    y3 = ( y1 + y2 ) / 2;
    g2d.drawString(wts, x3, y3);

    //draw the north-south arrow head
    x1 = x2 - 5;
    y1 = y2 - 5;
    x3 = x2 + 5;
    y3 = y2 - 5;
    g2d.drawLine(x1, y1, x2, y2);
    g2d.drawLine(x2, y2, x3, y3);
    g2d.setStroke(prevStk);
}

if(col < matrix[row].length - 1 && row != 0){

    x1 = x + width;
    y1 = y + (height/2);
    x2 = x + space ;
    y2 = y1;
    g2d.drawLine(x1, y1, x2, y2);
    //draw the west-east weights
    wts = String.valueOf( row_weights[row][col] );
    x3 = (( x1 + x2 ) / 2 ) - (wts.length()*2);
```

```
                              y3 = y1 - 10;
                        g2d.drawString(wts, x3, y3);
                              g2d.setStroke(prevStk);
            }

         }
                  else //draw the currentcell and get the
direction of the
                  //prevcell so we can draw arrows pointing to
it
                  //and then draw the score and the weights
            {
                        g2d.drawOval(x, y, width, height);
                        if(col < matrix[row].length - 1 ){

                        //now draw the west-east line
                        x1 = x + width;
                              y1 = y + (height/2);
                              x2 = x + space ;
                              y2 = y1;
                              g2d.drawLine(x1, y1, x2, y2);
                              //draw the west-east score
                              wts =
                              String.valueOf(
                        row_weights[row][col] );
                              x3 = (( x1 + x2 ) / 2 ) -
(wts.length()*2);
                              //x3 = x1 - wts.length();
                              y3 = y1 - 10;
                              g2d.drawString(wts, x3, y3);
                        }
                        //if the row is not 0 draw the north-
south line
                        if (row > 0){
                              //draw the north-south line
                                    x1 = x + (width/2);
                                    y1 = y - space + height;
                                    x2 = x1;
                                    y2 = y1 + space - height;
```

```
                        g2d.drawLine(x1, y1,
x2, y2);
                        //draw the north-south weights
                        wts =
                             String.valueOf(
                        col_weights[row-1][col] );
                        x3 = x1 + 10;
                        y3 = ( y1 + y2 ) / 2;
                        g2d.drawString(wts, x3, y3);
                    }
                //if the prev cell is above draw arrow
again with
                //bold stroke

                    if(prevCellMap.get(Constant.CE
                    LL_ABOVE) != null) {
                      x1 = x + (width/2);
                      y1 = y - space + height;
                      x2 = x1;
                      y2 = y1 + space - height;
                      g2d.setStroke(boldStk);
                      g2d.drawLine(x1, y1, x2, y2);
                      //draw the north-south arrow
head
                      x1 = x2 - 5;
                      y1 = y2 - 5;
                      x3 = x2 + 5;
                      y3 = y2 - 5;
                      g2d.drawLine(x1, y1, x2, y2);
                      g2d.drawLine(x2, y2, x3, y3);
                      g2d.setStroke(prevStk);
                    }

                    if(prevCellMap.get(Constant.CELL_TO
                    _LEFT) != null)
                      {
                         x1 = x;
                         y1 = y + (height/2);
                         x2 = x - space + height;
                         y2 = y1;
```

```
                        g2d.setStroke(boldStk);
                        g2d.drawLine(x1, y1, x2, y2);
                            //now draw the arrow heads
                            x2 = x1 - 5;
                            y2 = y1 - 5;
                            x3 = x1 - 5;
                            y3 = y1 + 5;
                            g2d.drawLine(x1, y1, x2, y2);
                            g2d.drawLine(x1, y1, x3, y3);
                            g2d.setStroke(prevStk);
                    }
                }

                    //draw the score
                    score =
String.valueOf(currentCell.getScore());
                    x1 = x + (width/2) - (score.length()*2);
                    y1 = y + (height/2);
                    g2d.drawString(score, x1, y1);
                    x += space;

                }
                if (row == 0)
                area.width += x;
                x = 30;
                y += space;

            }
    area.height = y;
        }
```

DISCUSSION

DPMax for Weights set out to implement an algorithm that solves the Manhattan Tourist Problem and more. It would also provide as many of the longest paths existing in the grid. If indeed there are 2 or more longest paths, it means the tourist can have the luxury of choosing only the very best attractions given the situation.

DPMax for Weights not only makes this task simple but also displays the one or more longest paths on a grid which can be examined visually or even printed out for future use and reference.

DPMax for Weights can be upgraded and modified to find important use in the following ways:

1. Transportation

The field of transportation can benefit greatly from the Weights algorithm. The algorithm can be used to find the longest paths between 2 points and use that calculation to create schedules for traveling, and for calculating costs for accounting and finance. This use is highlighted in the topic covered in this paper.

2. Travel and Tourism

The algorithm can also be used to create schedulers for the tourism industry. Travelers can use this schedule to build their personal tourism schedules in any region they visit. Airlines can compute the distances and time to travel those distances. This information can then be used to calculate the amount of fuel and other costs needed for travel. This use is also highlighted in the topic covered in this paper.

3. Construction and Civil Engineering

The Weights algorithm can be used in construction of infrastructure like bridges, passes and so on. There may be a need to find the paths in the building of these structures.

4. Economics, Business and Finance

Dynamic Programming by itself is an invaluable technique for numerous economics and finance procedures such as cost accounting, budgeting and profit and loss accounting. Furthermore, there is immense use of DP algorithms for computing largest and smallest costs (longest and shortest paths) in the daily, monthly and annual transactions of business ventures (Bradley et. al.).

5. Others

The algorithm can also be used in various industries to calculate correct spacing in manufacturing, construction, building, and so on.

The Shortest Paths Algorithm

This paper has looked at the problem of finding the longest paths between a start and finish points. But there is also the need to find the opposite: the shortest paths between 2 points on a grid. I shall call this problem the *Impatient Tourist Problem*, ITP. This problem is an implementation of the famous *Shortest Paths Problem*. It is about a tourist who is in a hurry to get from point A to point B but wishes to get through them in the shortest amount of time, thereby seeing the best possible attractions, but in the shortest time, and path, possible (Bradley et. al., Chapter 11).

The solution to this problem is quite simple, considering we have gone through the algorithm for the longest paths problem. It must be noted that the ITP is by no means the same thing as the Traveling Salesman Problem, which goes through all cities without repetition and returns to the starting city (Reingold et. al.). ITP is simply the Manhattan Tourist, but instead of doing the maximum between two paths, it seeks the minimum between the 2 possible paths. The ITP has the same number of subproblems as the MTP, given the same number of rows and columns. This means that it will have the same number and weights of its edges, west-east and north-south, as the MTP. It will build the very same grid structure as the longest path problem it solved. And it will create the same number of vertices as the longest path problem, LPP. It solves the same grid, but it solves the decision variables at each stage of solving a subproblem slightly differently. It performs a minimum operation at each stage, rather than a maximum one. That is, it computes the value of the vertex, and path, that is smaller, rather than bigger, unlike the LPP.

So, the algorithm to find the shortest paths between source and vertex is an expected modification of the MTP. The difference is shown on line (6).

function ImpatientTourist()

To Find: The shortest paths between 2 points on a grid (Graph) of intersecting edges and vertices.

H[] – A 2-Dimensional array of weights of edges that run from west to east (horizontal)

V[] – A 2-Dimensional array of weights of edges that run from north to south (vertical)

n = length of the array *H[]*

m = length of the array *V*[]

(1) $G[0, 0] = 0$

(2)   for i = 0 to n

   $G[i, 0] = G[i-1, 0] + V[i, 0]$

(3)   for j = 0 to n

   $G[0, j] = G[j-1, 0] + H[0, j]$

(4)   for i = 1 to n

(5)   for j = 1 to m

(6) $L_{i,j} = \min(L_{i-1,j} + V[i, j], L_{i, j-1} + H[i, j])$

(7)   return $L_{n, m}$

IMPROVEMENTS

The improvements to the DPMax for Weights program are the same as its LCS counterpart, which have been discussed in the LCS paper.

ACKNOWLEDGEMENT

All supporting documents including the free copies of the thesis in this book in Word document format, all source code and binaries can be found online at the GitHub repository of this project, DPMax at:

https://github.com/ccolossus/DPMax

The author can be contacted at the following email:

cac.colossus@yahoo.com

CITATIONS

Baase, Sara, and Allen Van Gelder. Computer Algorithms: Introduction to Design and Analysis. 3rd ed., Addison-Wesley Longman, 2000.

Baxevanis, Andreas D., and B. F. Francis Ouellette, editors. *Bioinformatics: A Practical Guide to the Analysis of Genes and Proteins.* 3rd ed, Wiley, 2005.

Bellman, Richard, and Stuart Dreyfus. *Dynamic Programming.* 1. Princeton Landmarks in Mathematics ed., With a new introduction, Princeton University Press, 2010.

Bradley, Stephen P., et al. Applied Mathematical Programming. Addison-Wesley Pub. Co, 1977.

Chong, Jike, et al. *Dynamic Programming Pattern.* https://patterns.eecs.berkeley.edu/?page_id=416. Accessed Apr. 2009.

Cooper, Leon, and Mary W. Cooper. *Introduction to Dynamic Programming.* 1st ed, Pergamon Press, 1981.

Cormen, Thomas H., editor. *Introduction to Algorithms.* 3rd ed, MIT Press, 2009.

Dasgupta, Sanjoy, et. al. *Algorithms*. McGraw-Hill Higher Education, 2008.

Denardo, Eric V. *Dynamic Programming: Models and Applications*. Dover Publications, 2003.

GeeksforGeeks. *Overlapping Subproblems Property in Dynamic Programming | DP-1* https://www.geeksforgeeks.org/overlapping-subproblems-property-in-dynamic-programming-dp-1/. Accessed November 13, 2018.

Mount, David W. *Bioinformatics: Sequence and Genome Analysis*. 2nd ed, Cold Spring Harbor Laboratory Press, 2004.

Needleman, S. B., and C. D. Wunsch. "A General Method Applicable to the Search for Similarities in the Amino Acid Sequence of Two Proteins." *Journal of Molecular Biology*, vol. 48, no. 3, Mar. 1970, pp. 443–53.

Reingold, Edward M., et al. *Combinatorial Algorithms: Theory and Practice*. Prentice-Hall, 1977.

Smith, T. F., and M. S. Waterman. "Identification of Common Molecular Subsequences." *Journal of Molecular Biology*, vol. 147, no. 1, Mar. 1981, pp. 195–97.

Skiena, Steven S. *The Algorithm Design Manual.* 2nd ed, Springer, 2010.

Appendix A

Longest Path (Manhattan Tourist) Problem Through a 5x5 grid matrix

1. Input tab

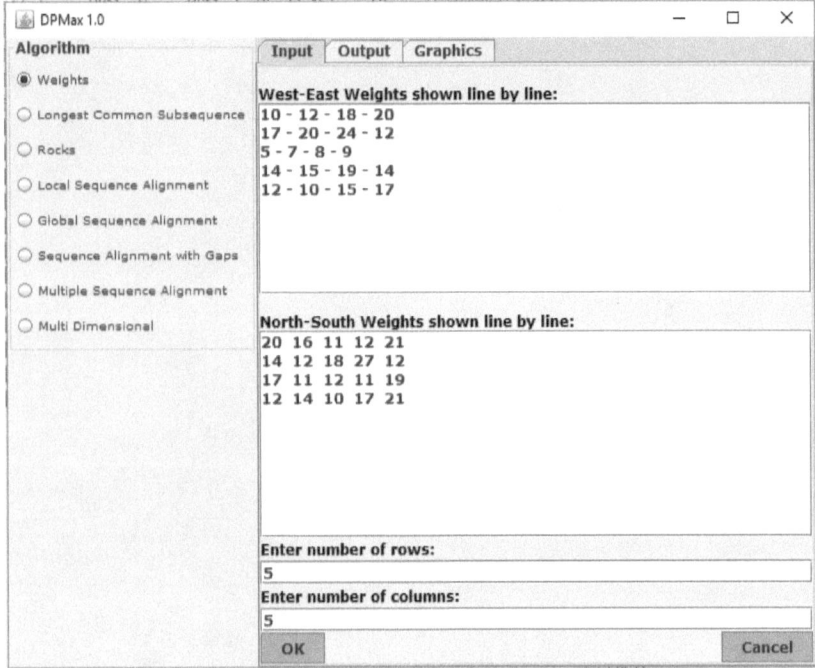

2. Output tab

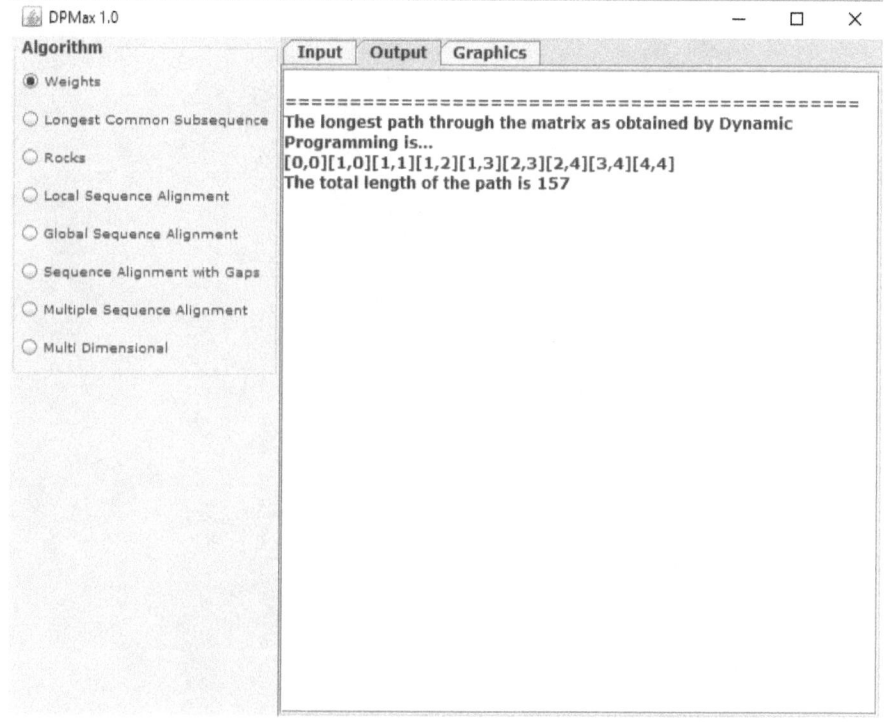

3. Graphics tab

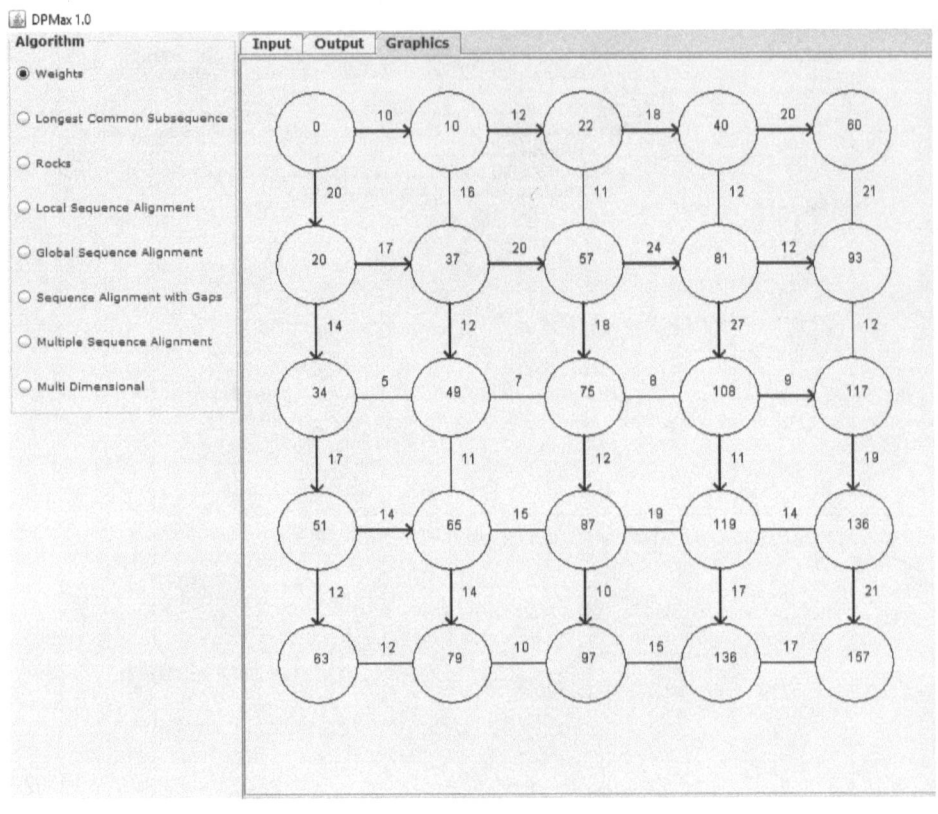

www.ingramcontent.com/pod-product-compliance
Lightning Source LLC
Chambersburg PA
CBHW021436210526
45463CB00002B/536